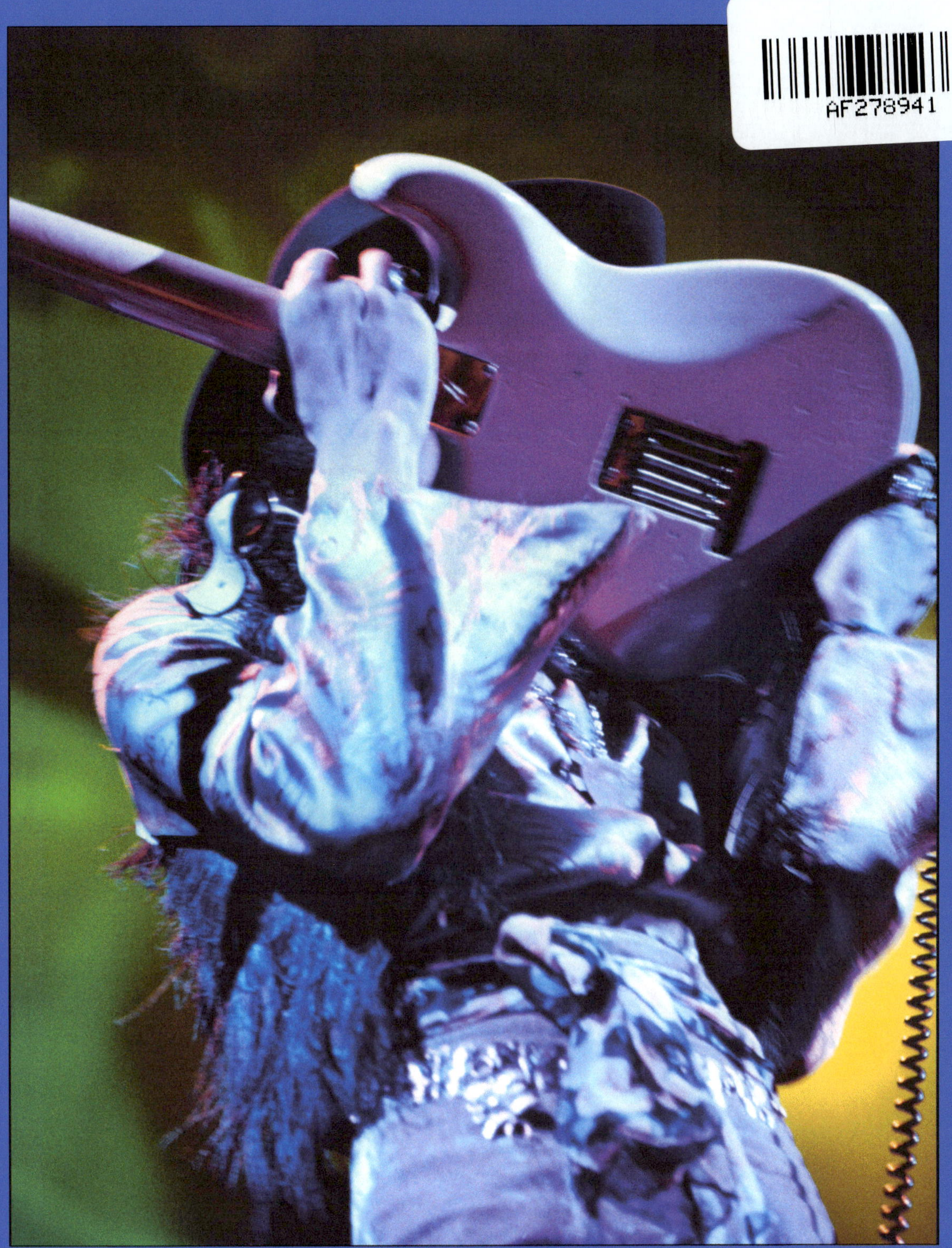

Elliott Landy's
Jimi Hendrix

Photos by Elliott Landy
text by Elliott Landy, Al Aronowitz, Tommy Fuller
www.elliottlandy.com

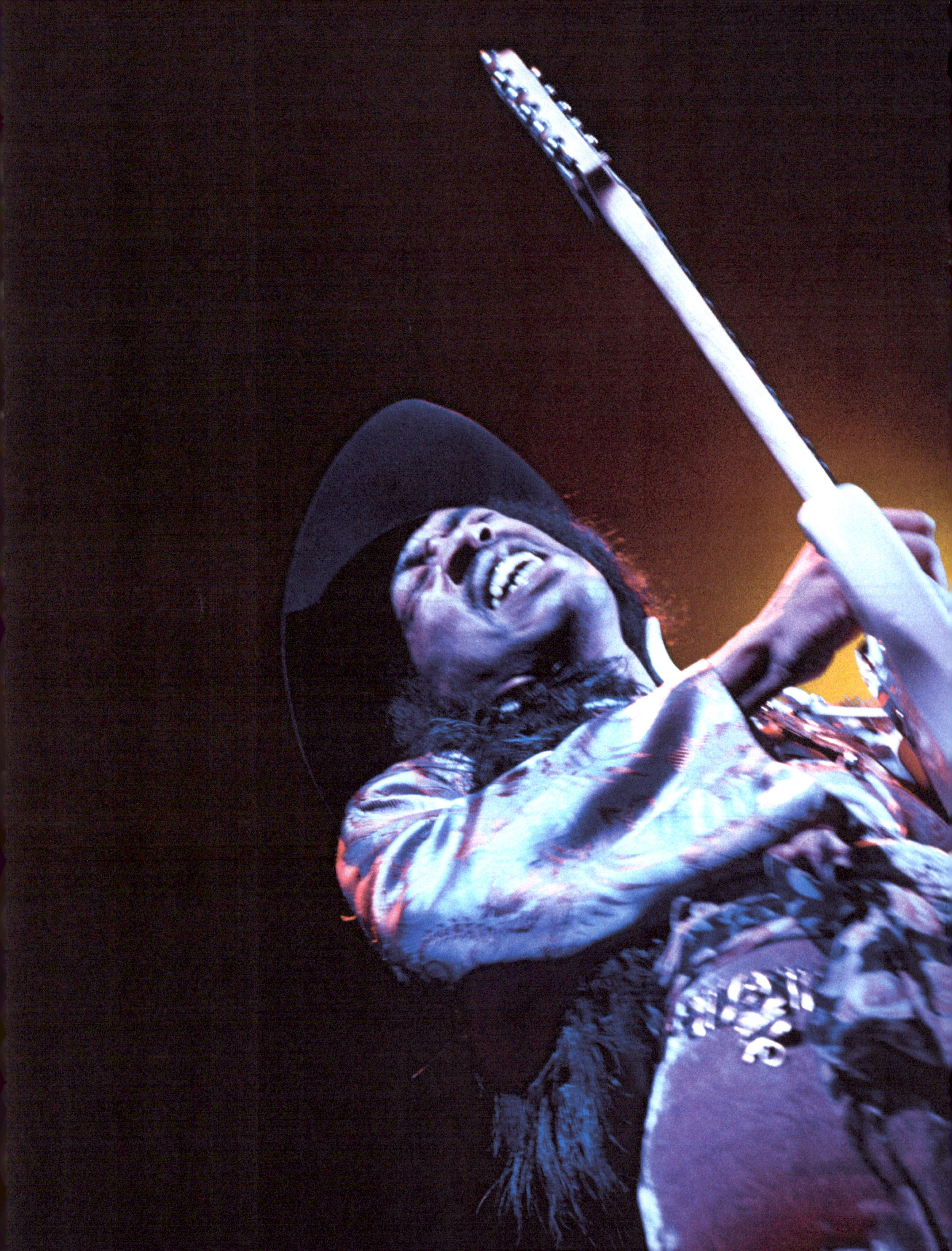

Taking Pictures of Jimi
Elliott Landy

On January 30, 1968, Jimi, Noel Redding and Mitch Mitchel (The Jimi Hendrix Experience) flew from London to NY and held a press conference at the top of the Pan Am building. This was Jimi's first time back in USA after becoming a superstar in UK. I sat alongside my friend Al Aronowitz, a well known music journalist. while he interviewed Jimi, and took a few photos discreetly, taking care not to disturb the flow of their conversation. I hadn't met Jimi, nor seen him play. Thinking back, it's pretty interesting to realize that the first time i saw him I was sitting across a table listening to him talk about his life and work in a very personal way. It felt like we knew each other—he was so open and gracious. He was real, he was present and conscious of what was going on around him, yet entirely unaffected by it. Nor was he demeaning the near chaotic, somewhat comic situation of the press crunch around him. He was grooving on it all, enjoying it. He was a nice, very gentle man. He was having fun taking pictures of the photographers taking pictures of him. I have been told that his film has gotten lost. He used to shoot Super 8 film everywhere he went.

I was photographing for Underground newspapers at the time (The Rat, Subterranean News, The New York Free Press.) Nearly all of the press were from major media—New York Times, Daily News, Associated Press. I didn't know who he was and hadn't heard any of his music yet.

On May 10, 1968, I was photographing at the Fillmore East and Jimi was the second act. I had photographed a very long set by Sly and The Family Stone and was really tired and exhausted so I decided to go home, telling myself that I would "get him another time." I didn't feel like carrying my heavy cameras around and going through the physical exertion of taking any more photographs that night.

I packed my two bags of cameras and headed towards the rear exit. Just as I was about to leave—I had my hand on the door—I heard Hendrix start to play. I was transfixed and then walked back into the auditorium and stood for a while behind the seated audience. I took one camera and took a few shots and then, despite my exhaustion, I took out all my cameras, slung them over my shoulder and walked back down to the front of the stage to photograph the set. The sound was so powerful, I couldn't resist.

I'm really glad I did. Because after that, I had no other chance. There were times when I could have. I was in NYC on New Year's Eve when he played with Buddy Miles, and I was at Woodstock but didn't stay for the last morning. I expected him to go on forever and kept thinking I would get him another day.

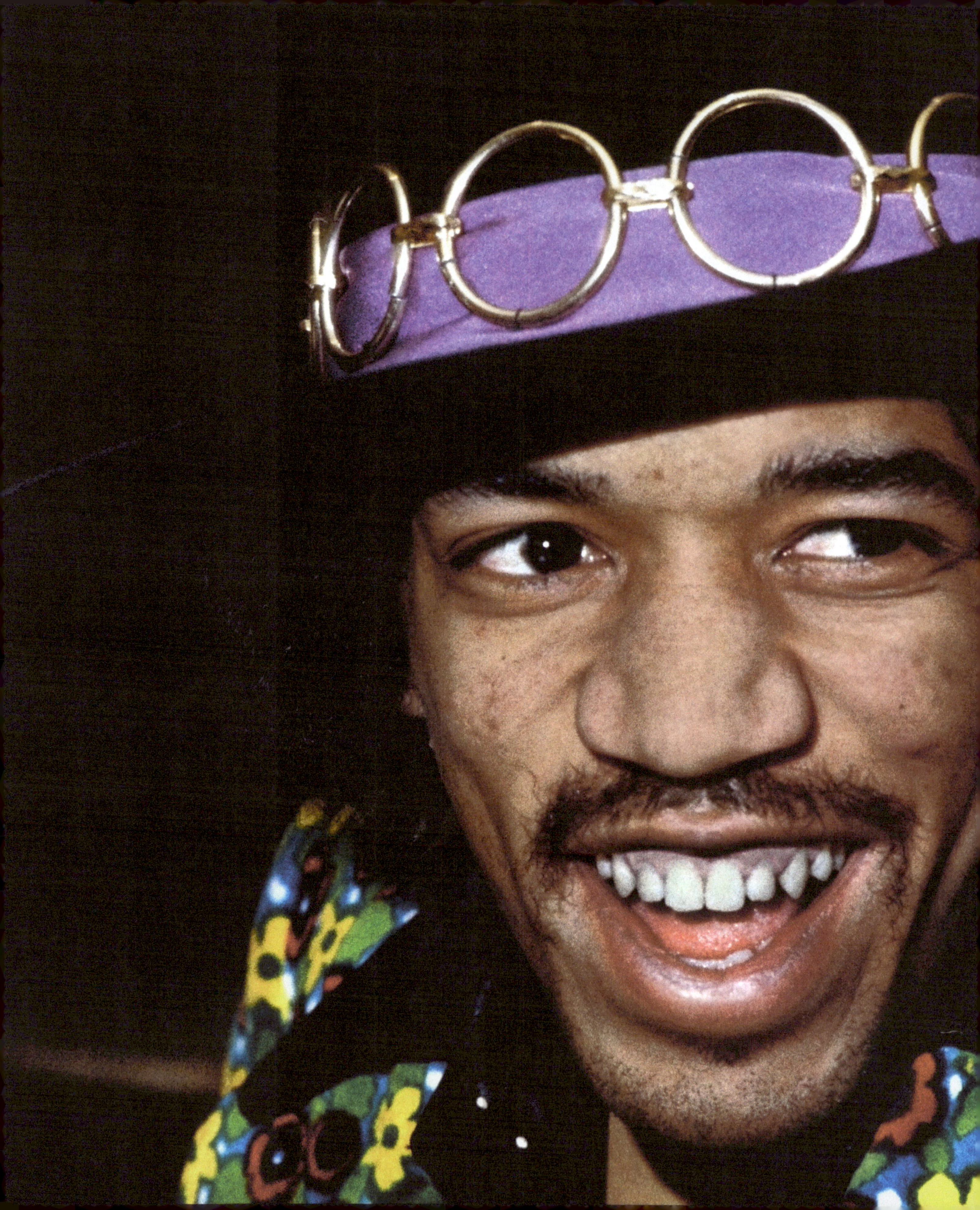

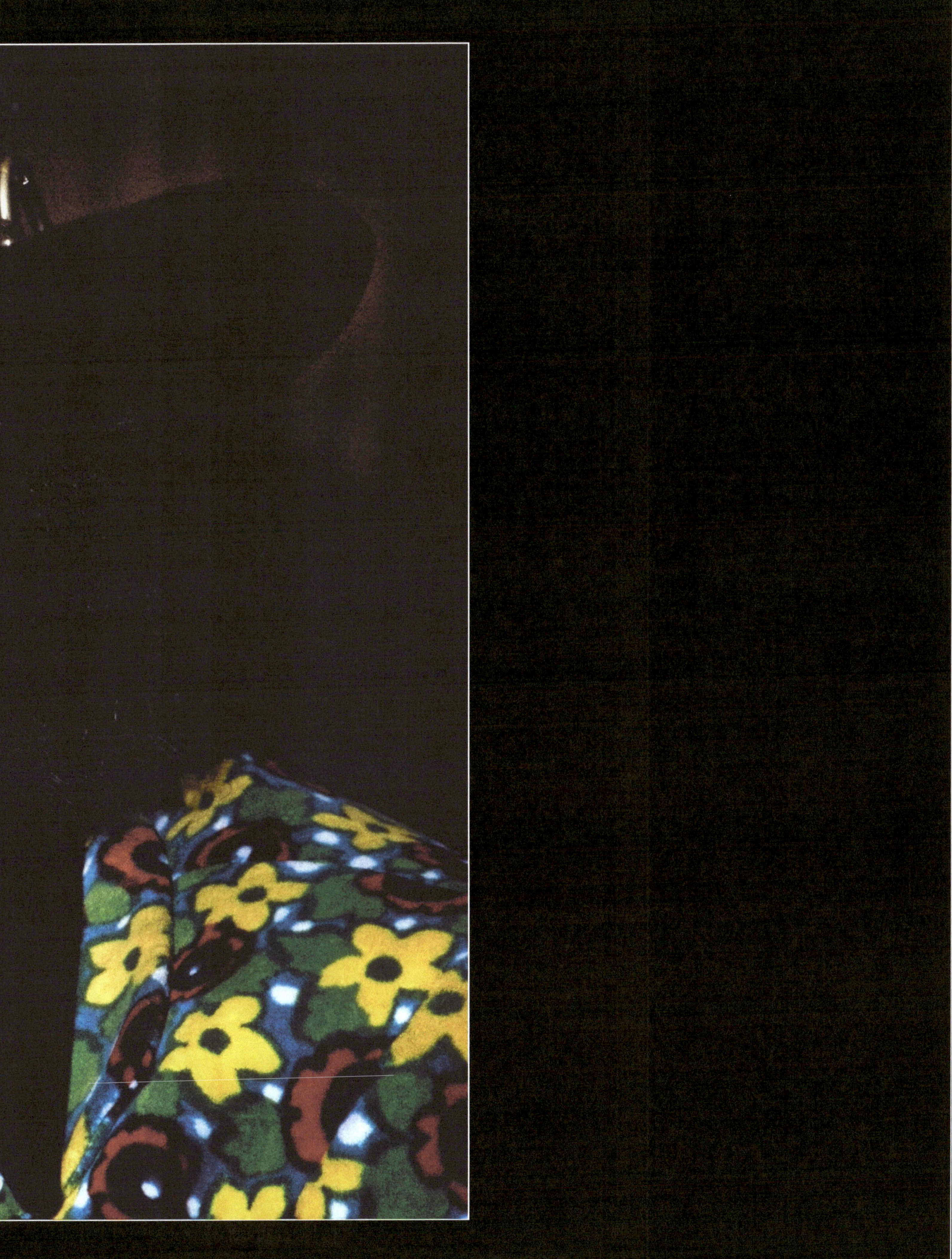

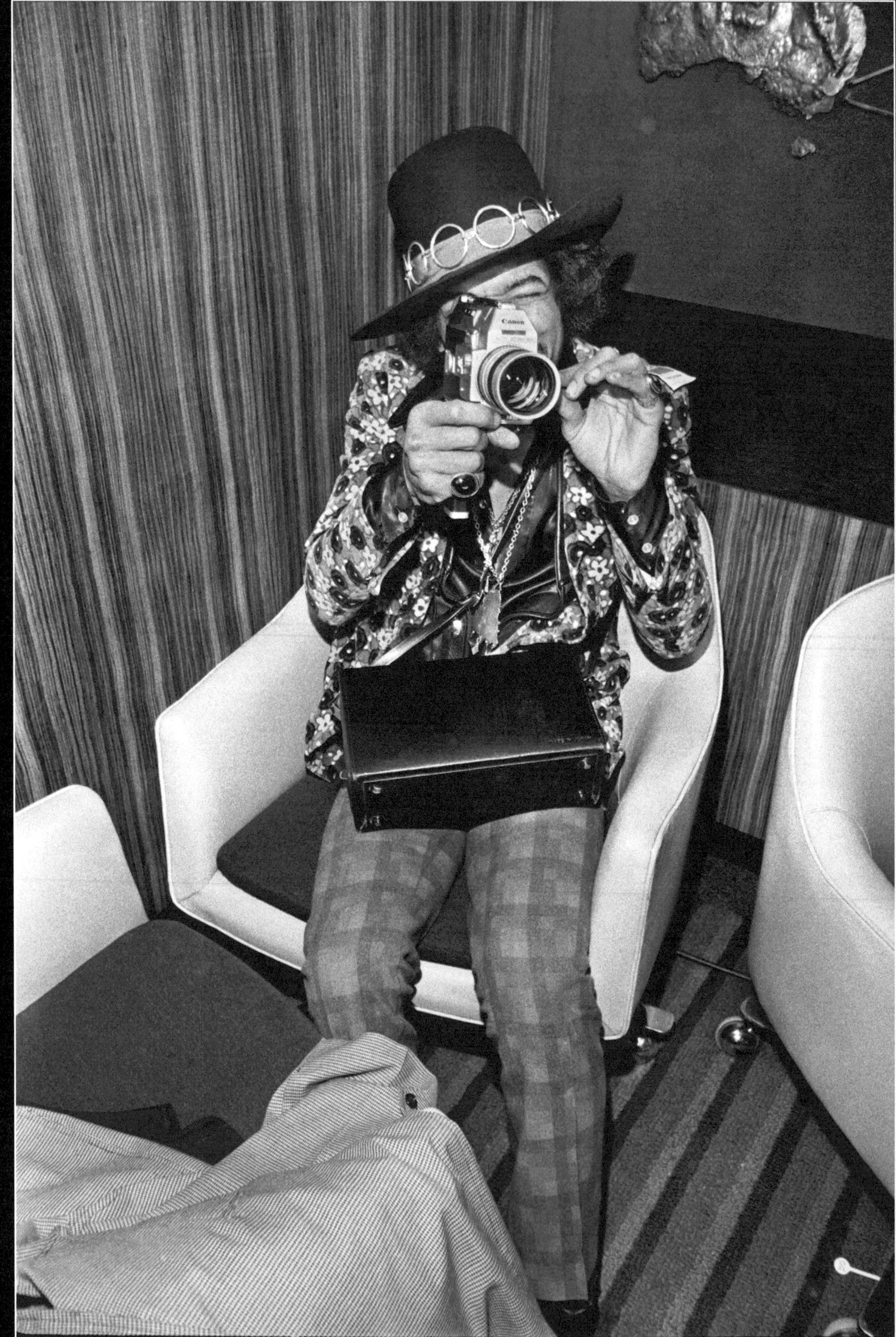

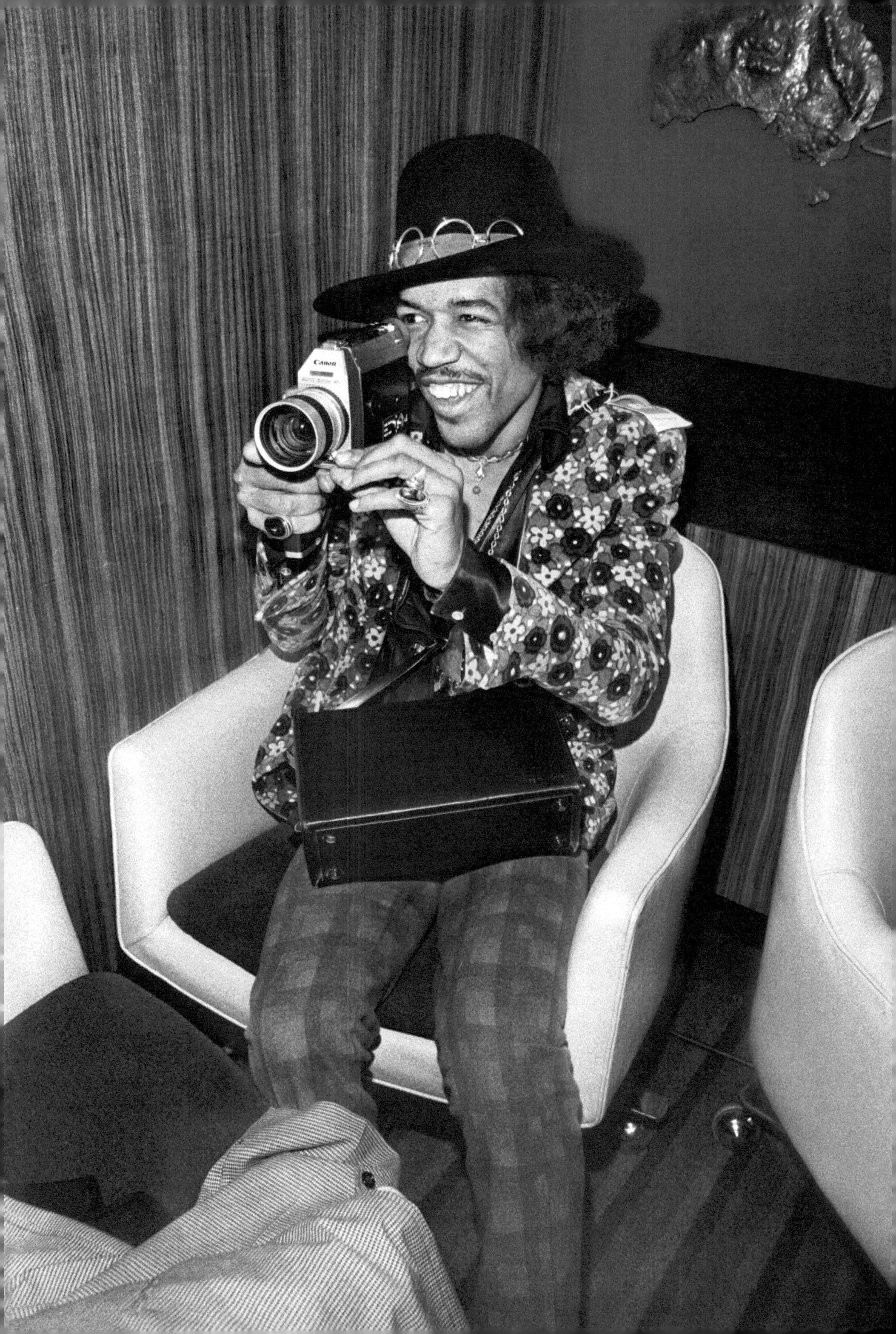

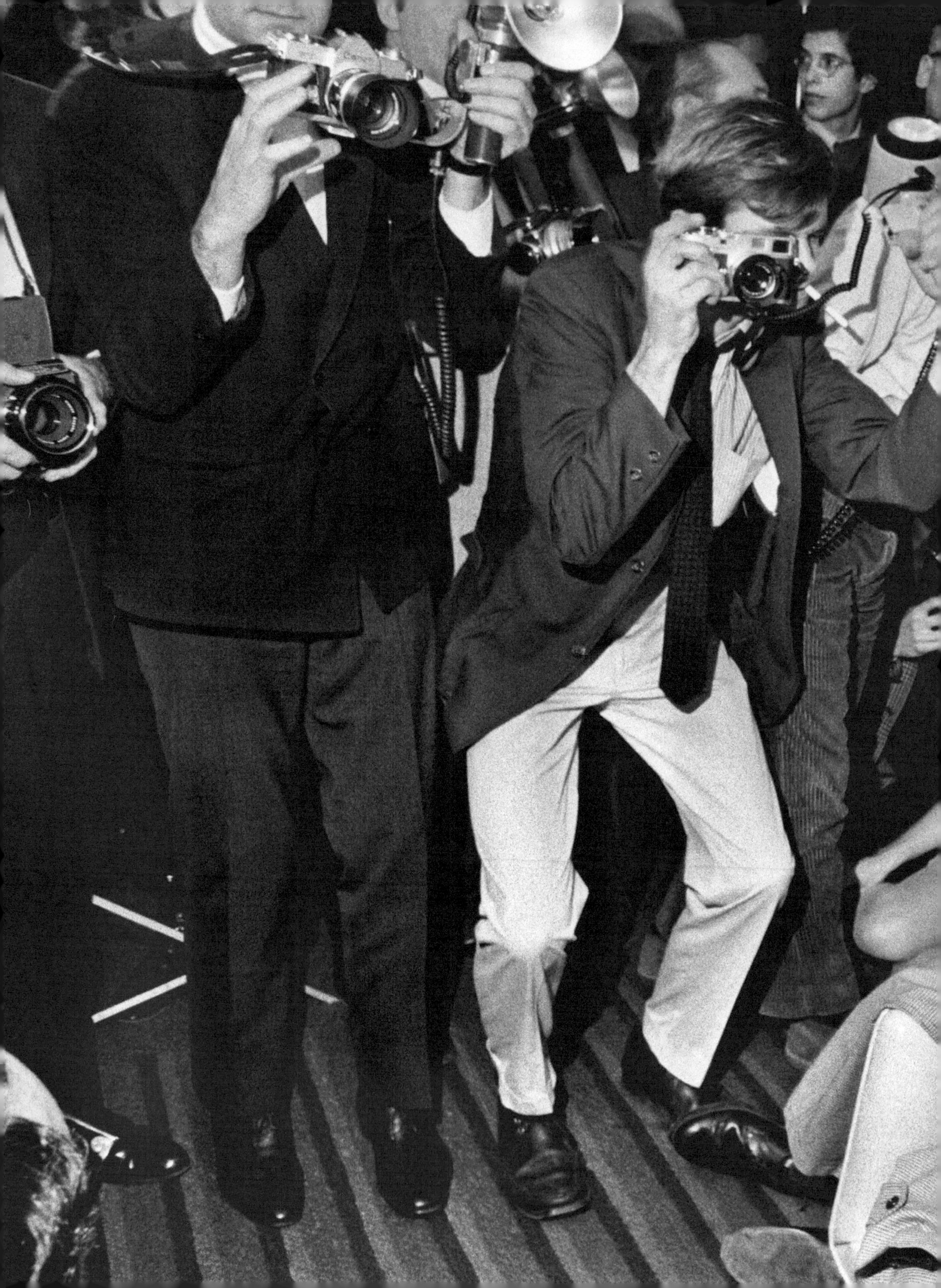

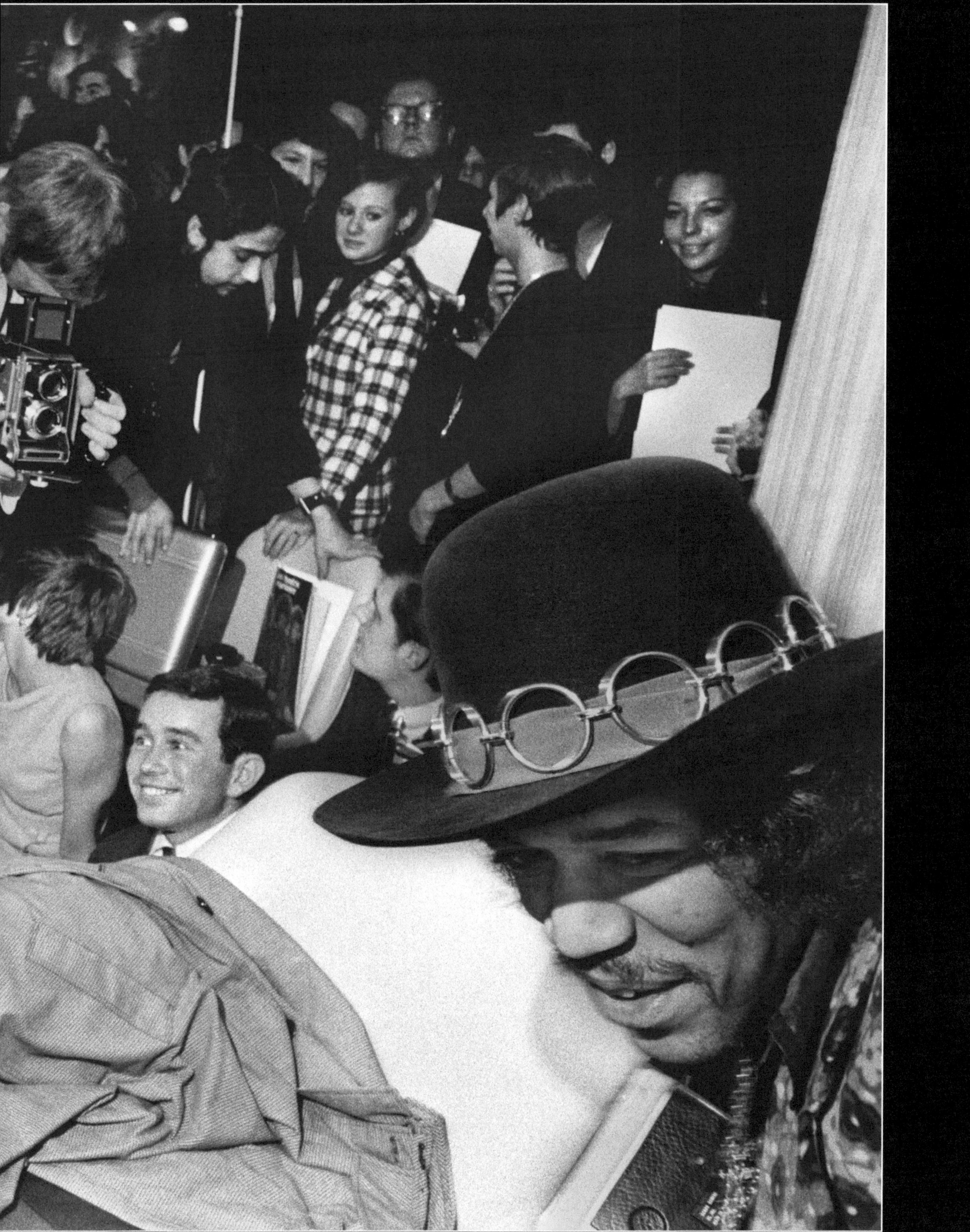

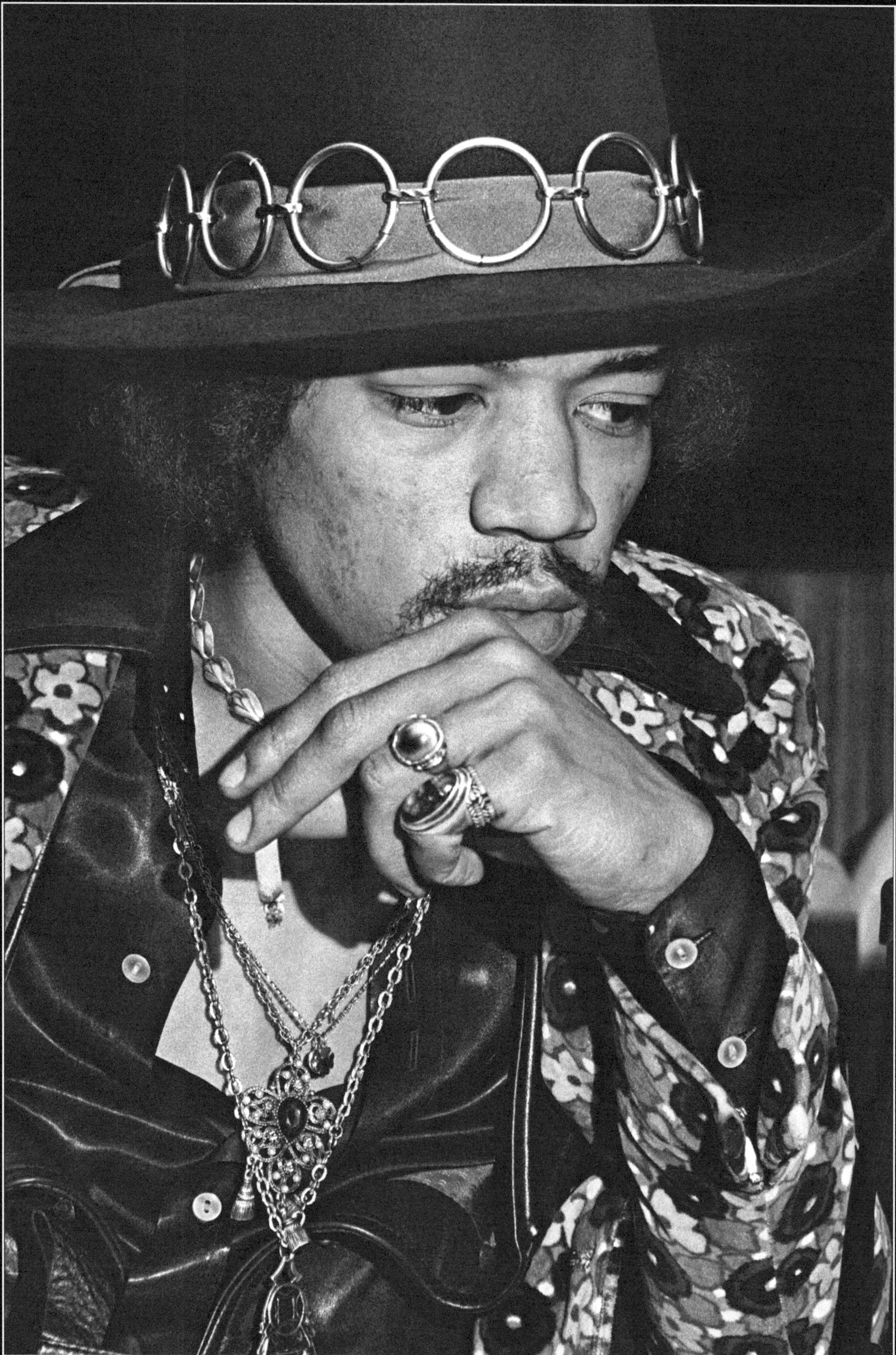

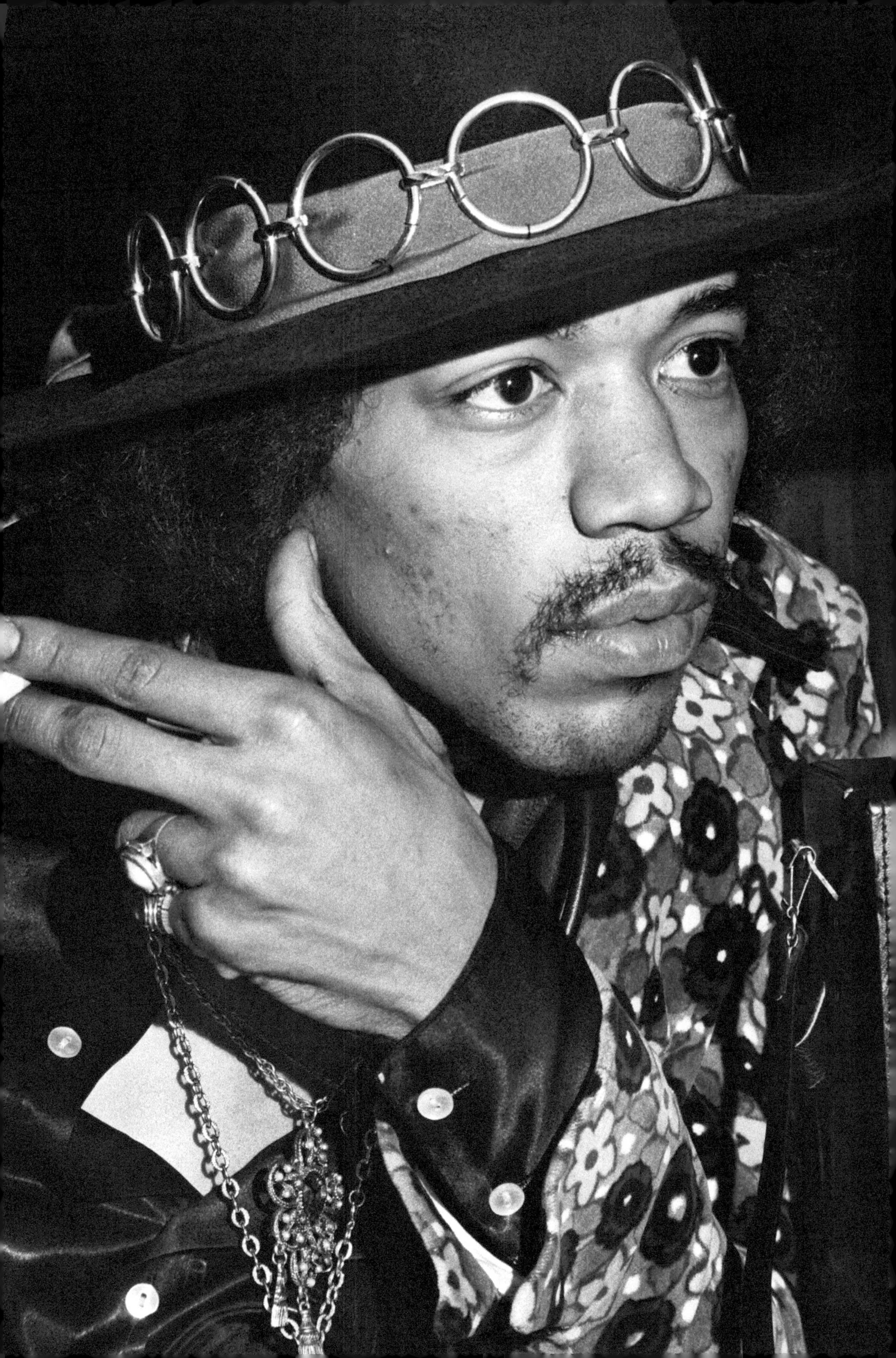

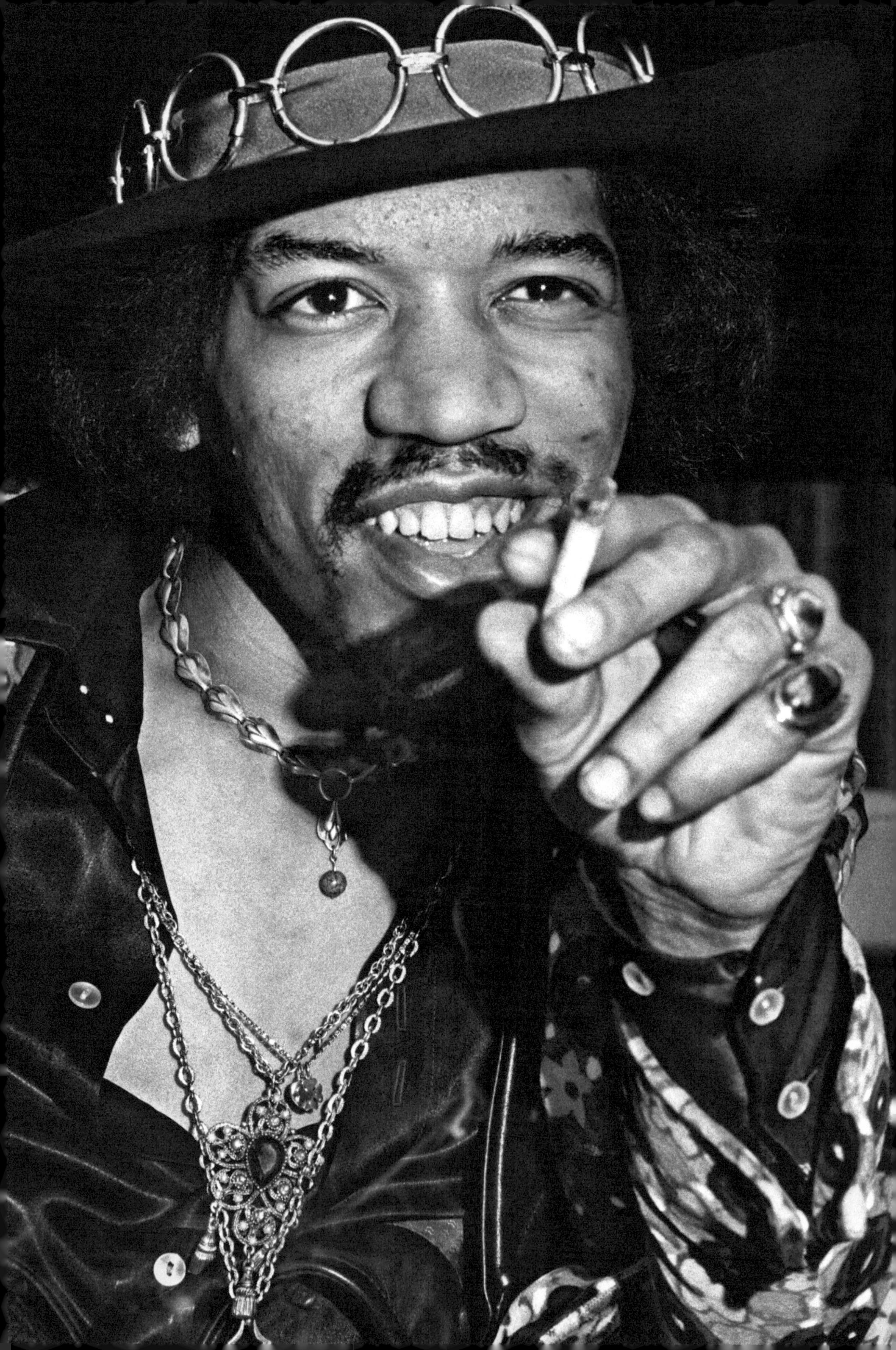

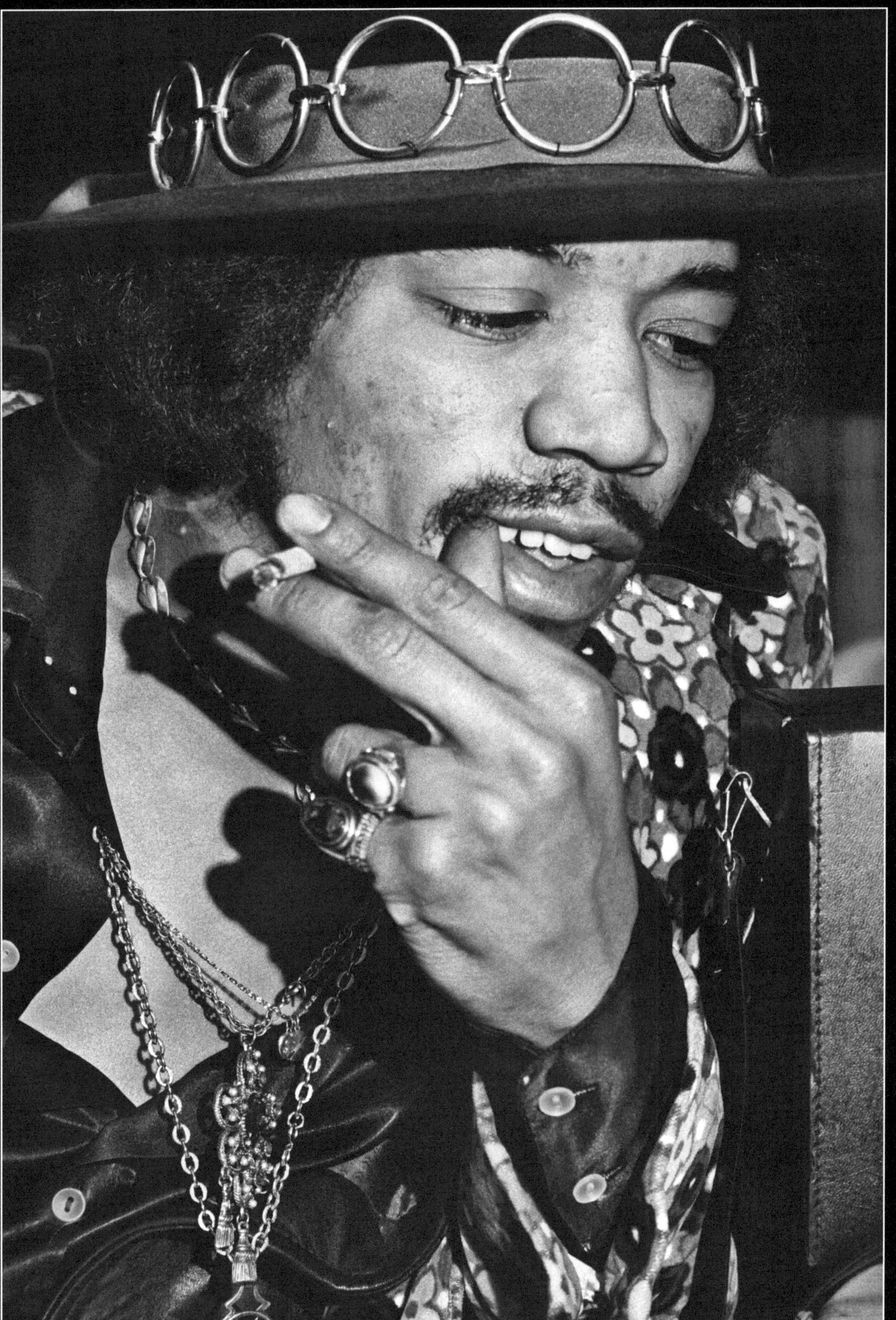

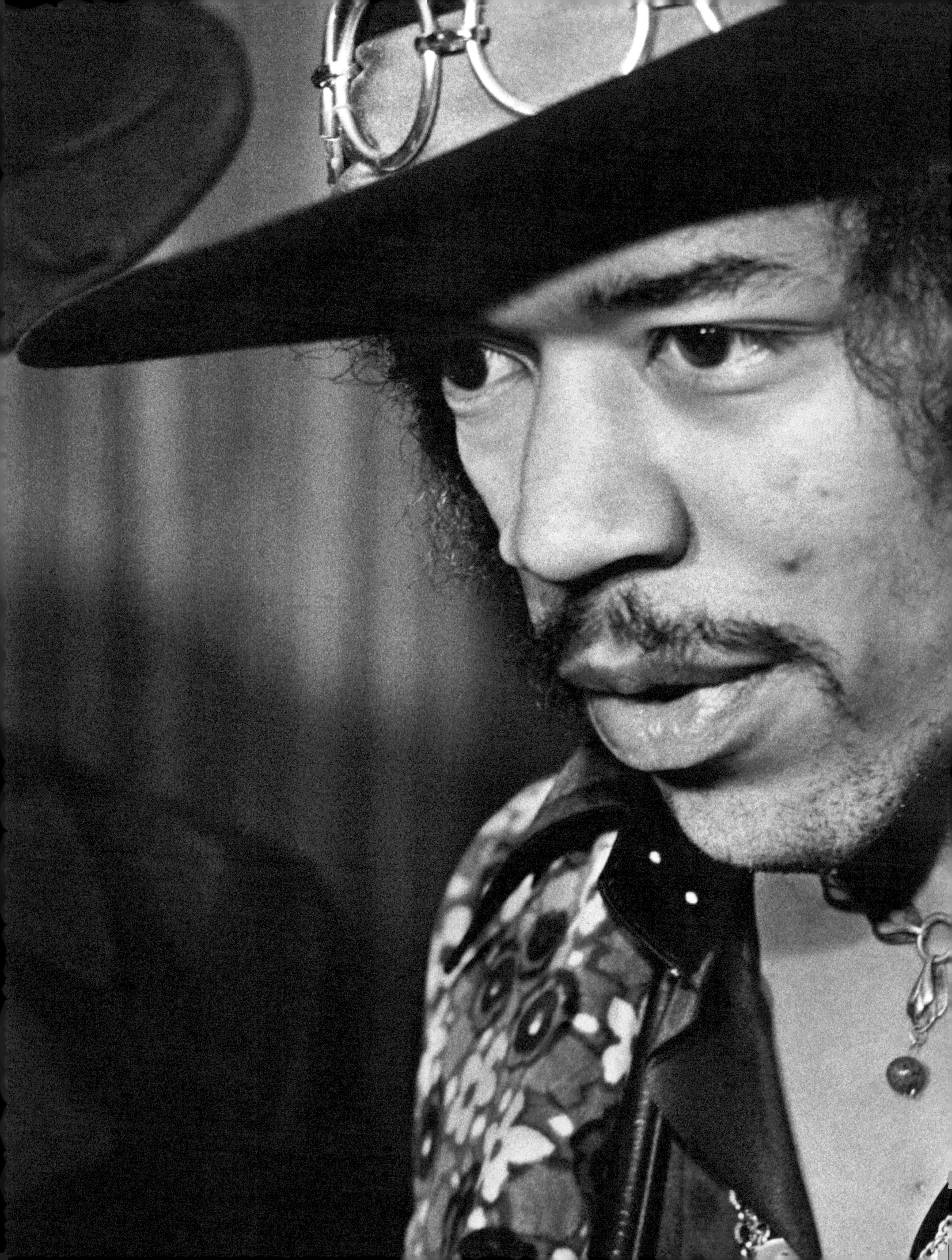

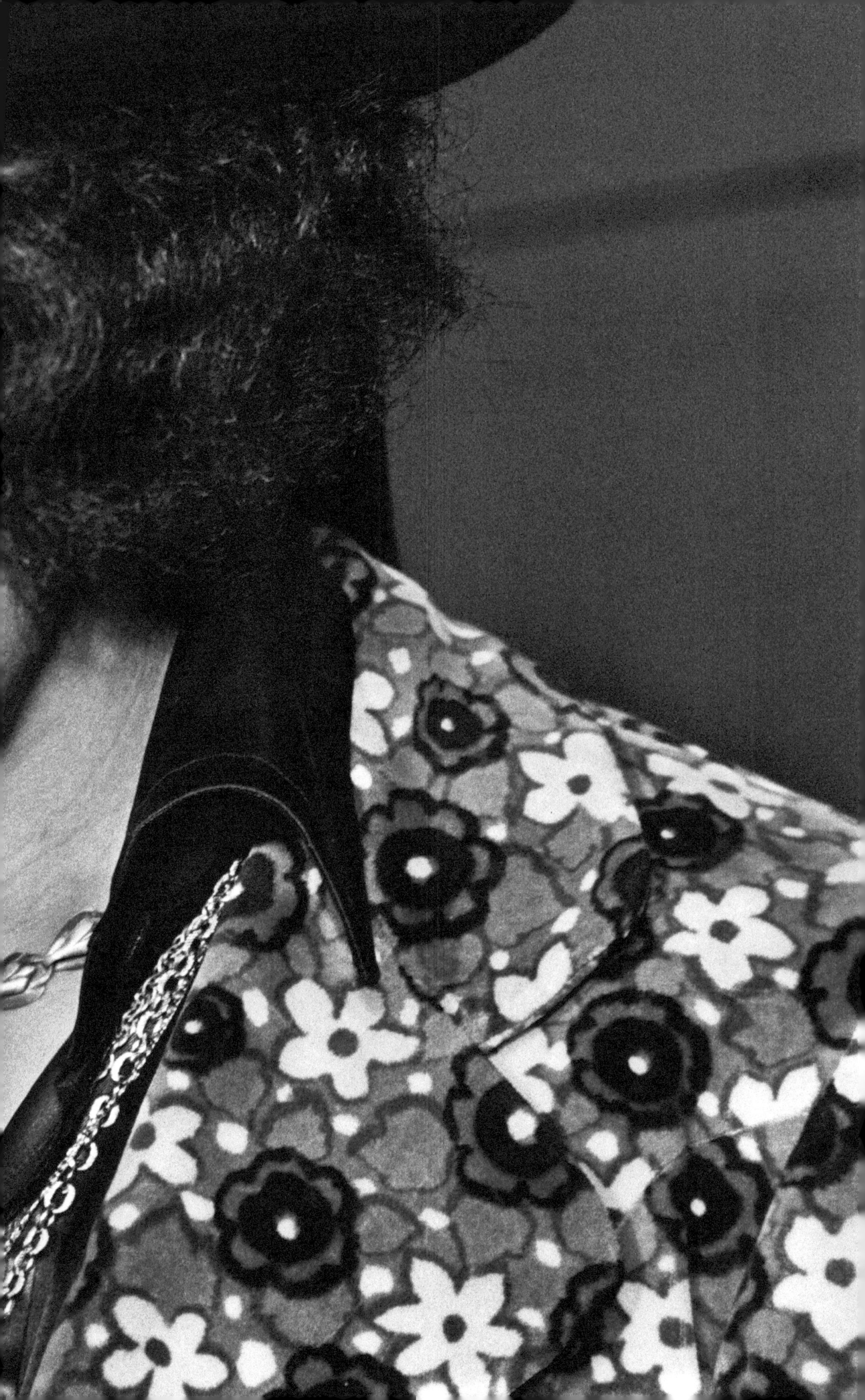

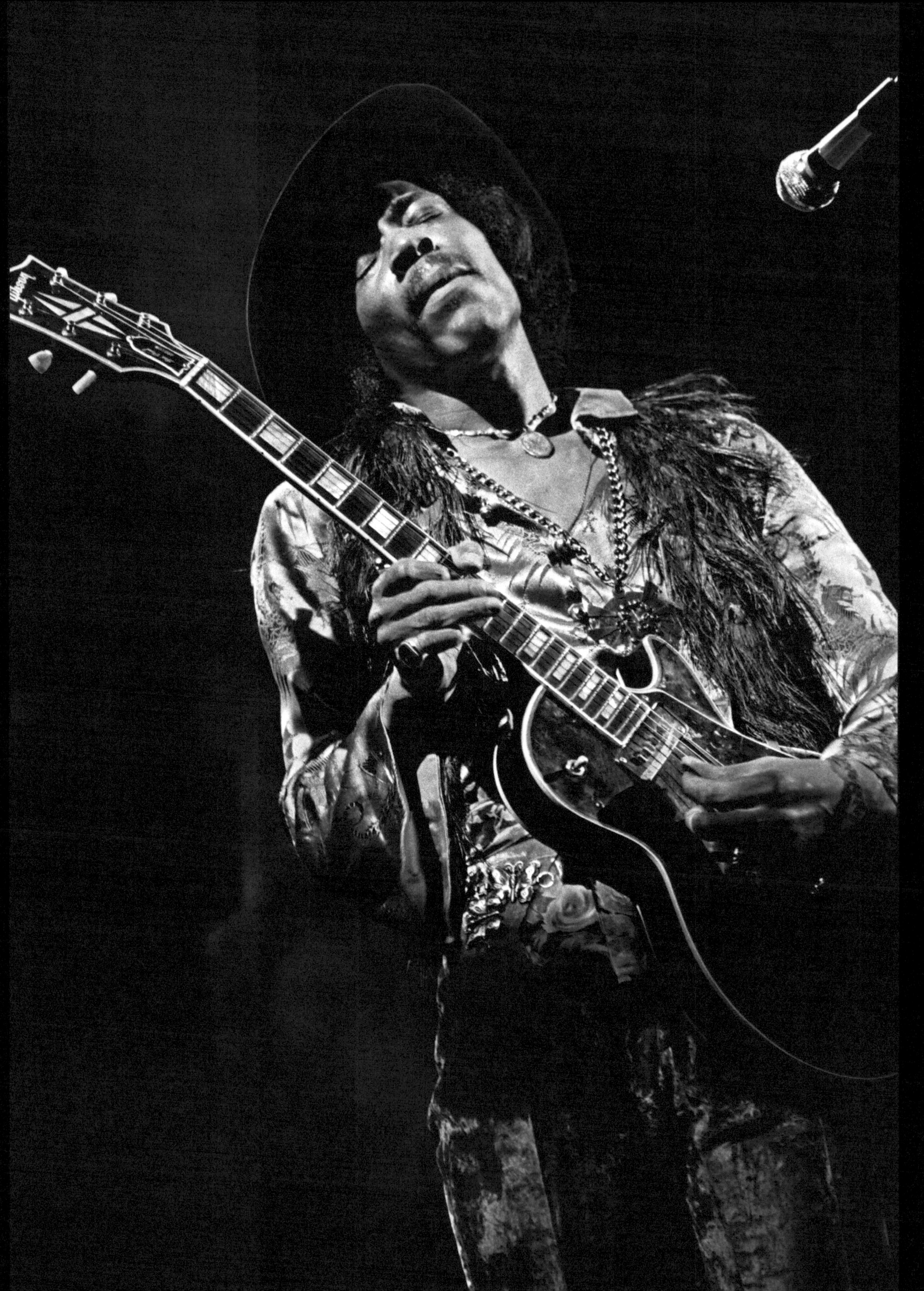

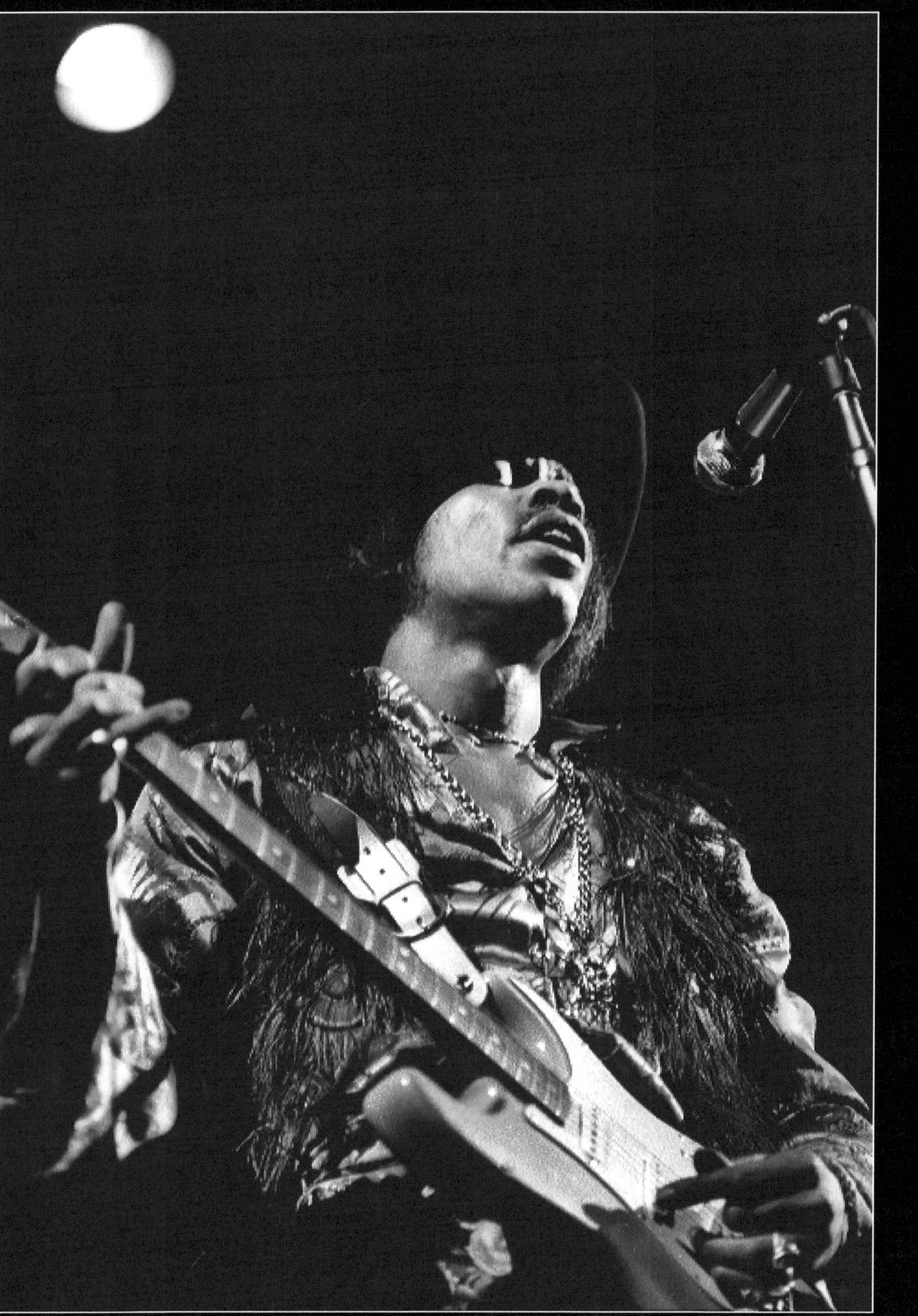

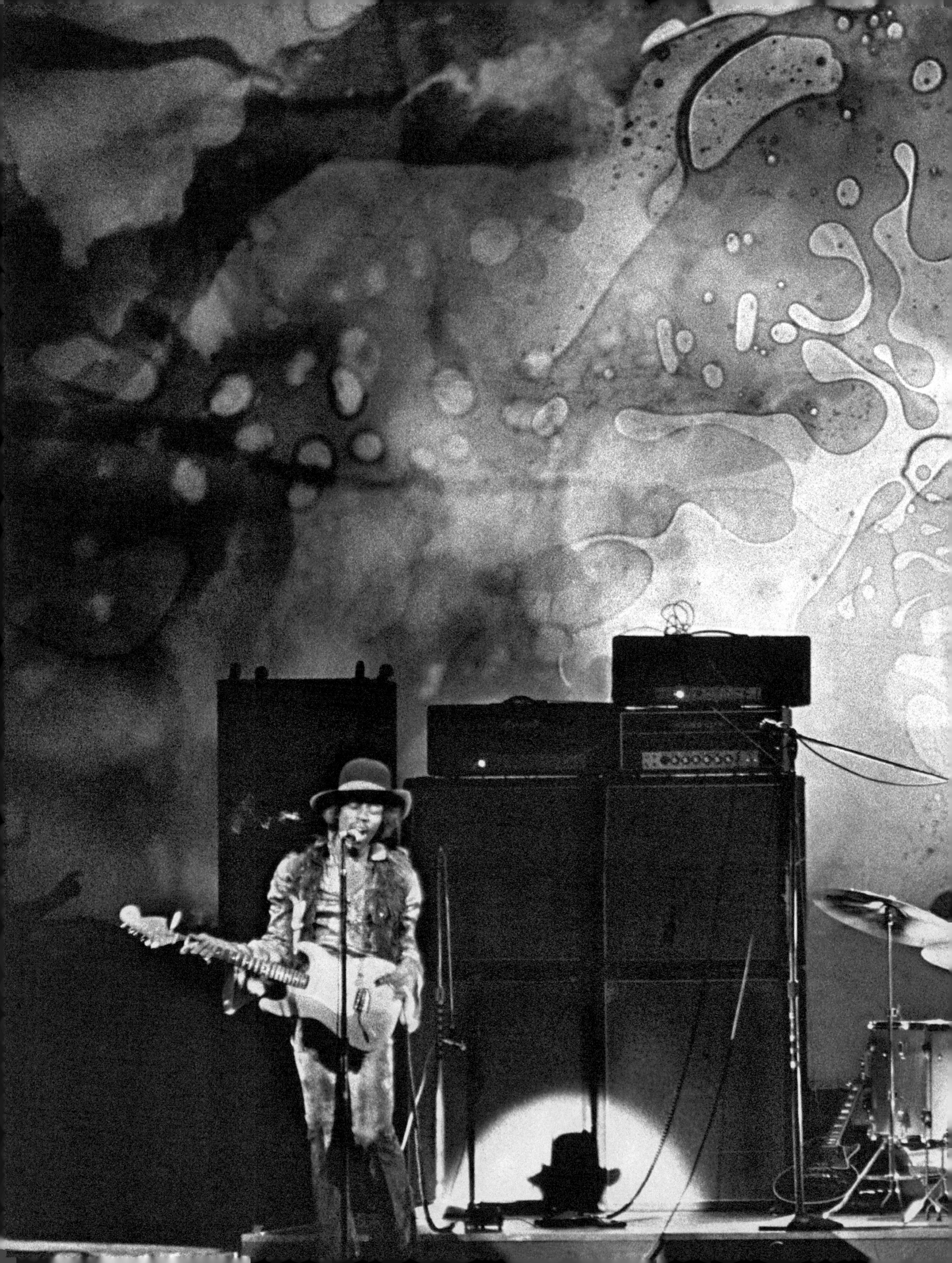

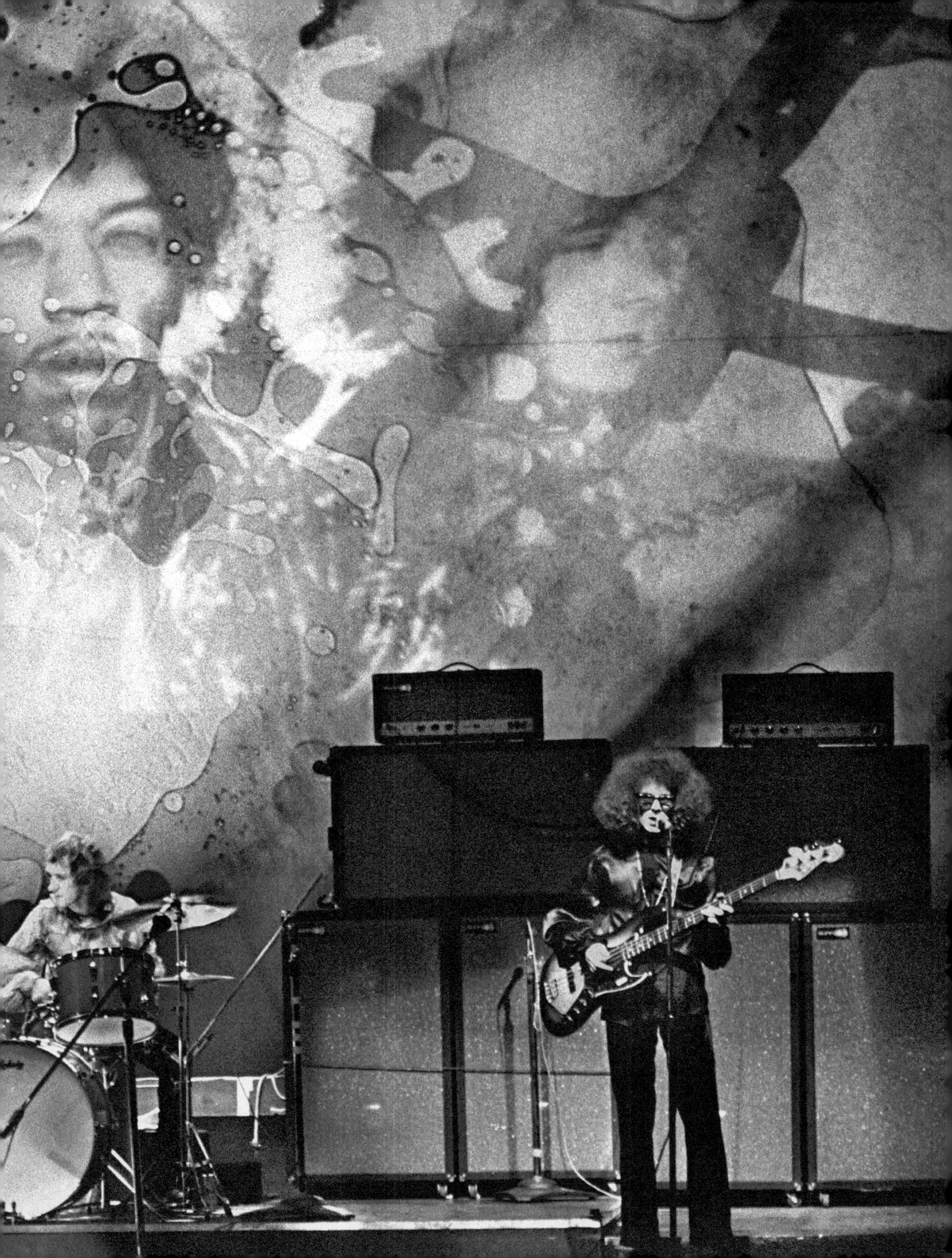

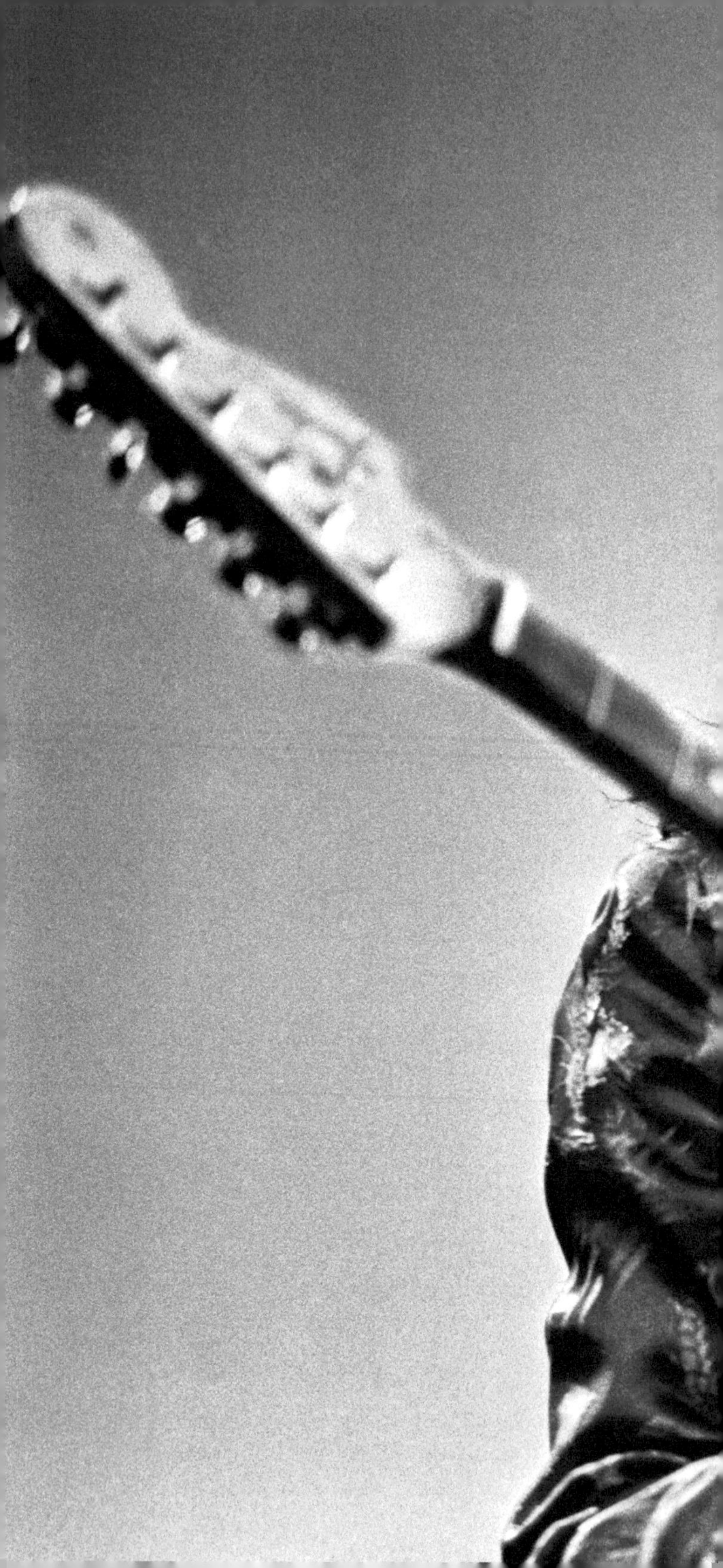

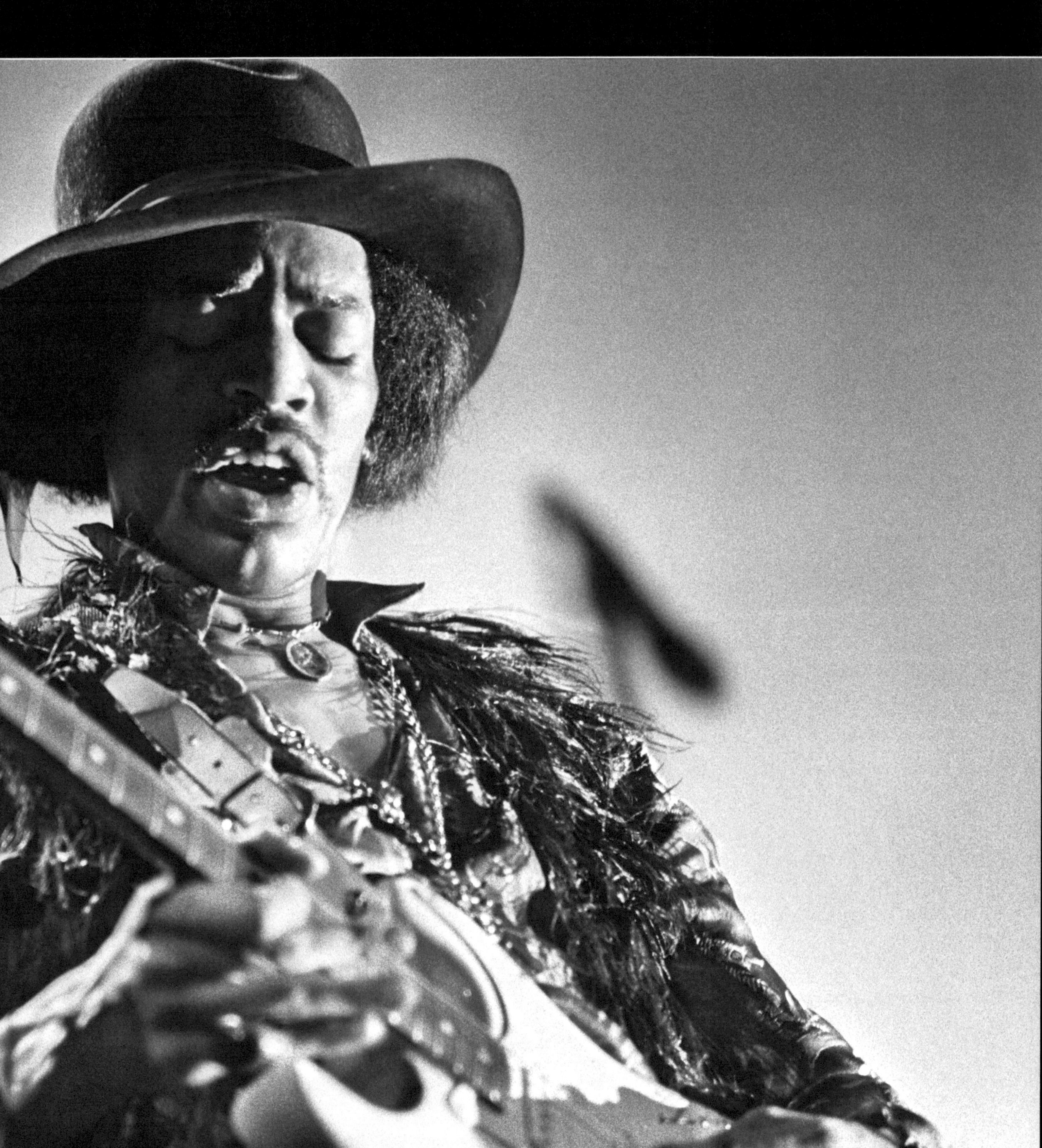

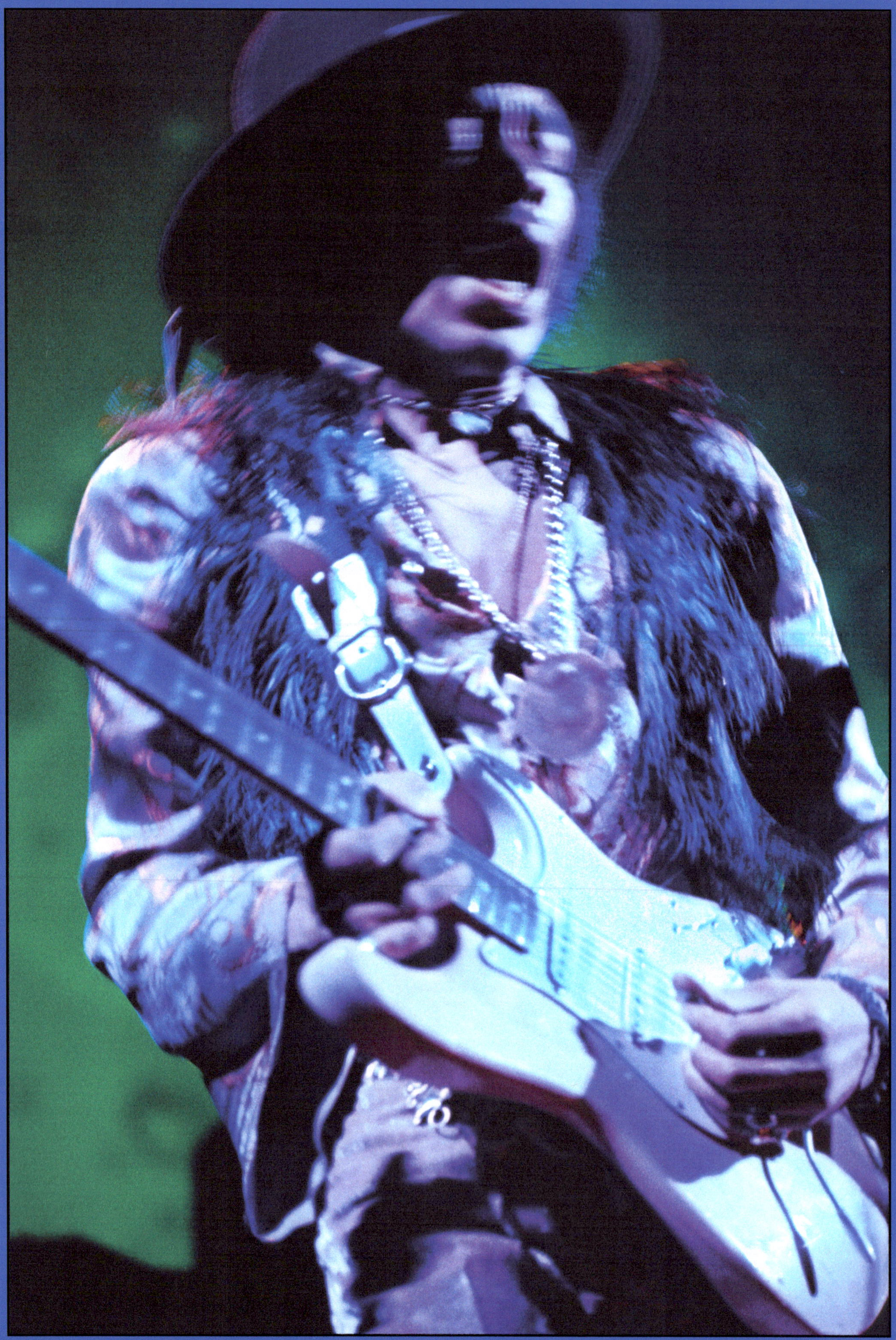

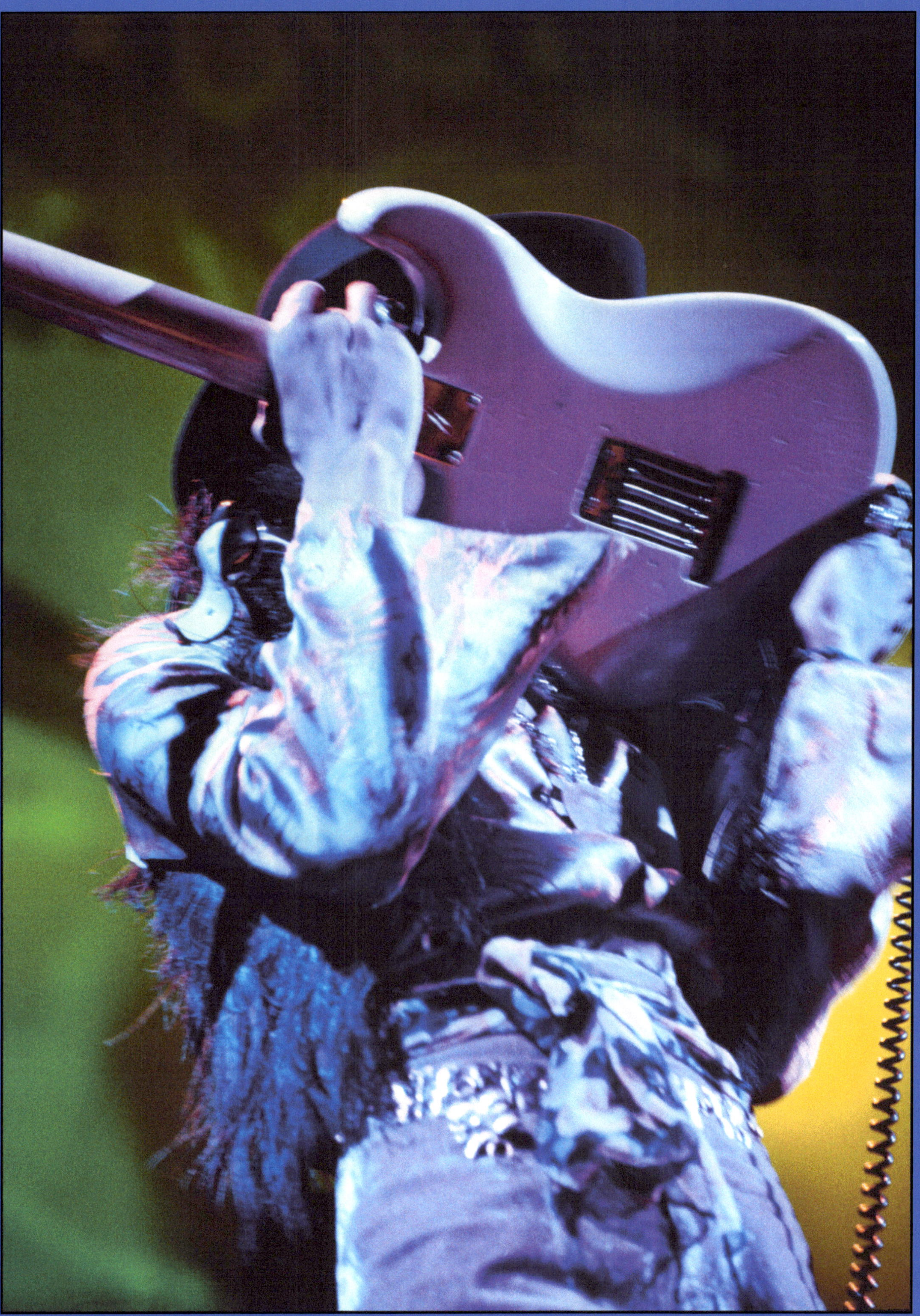

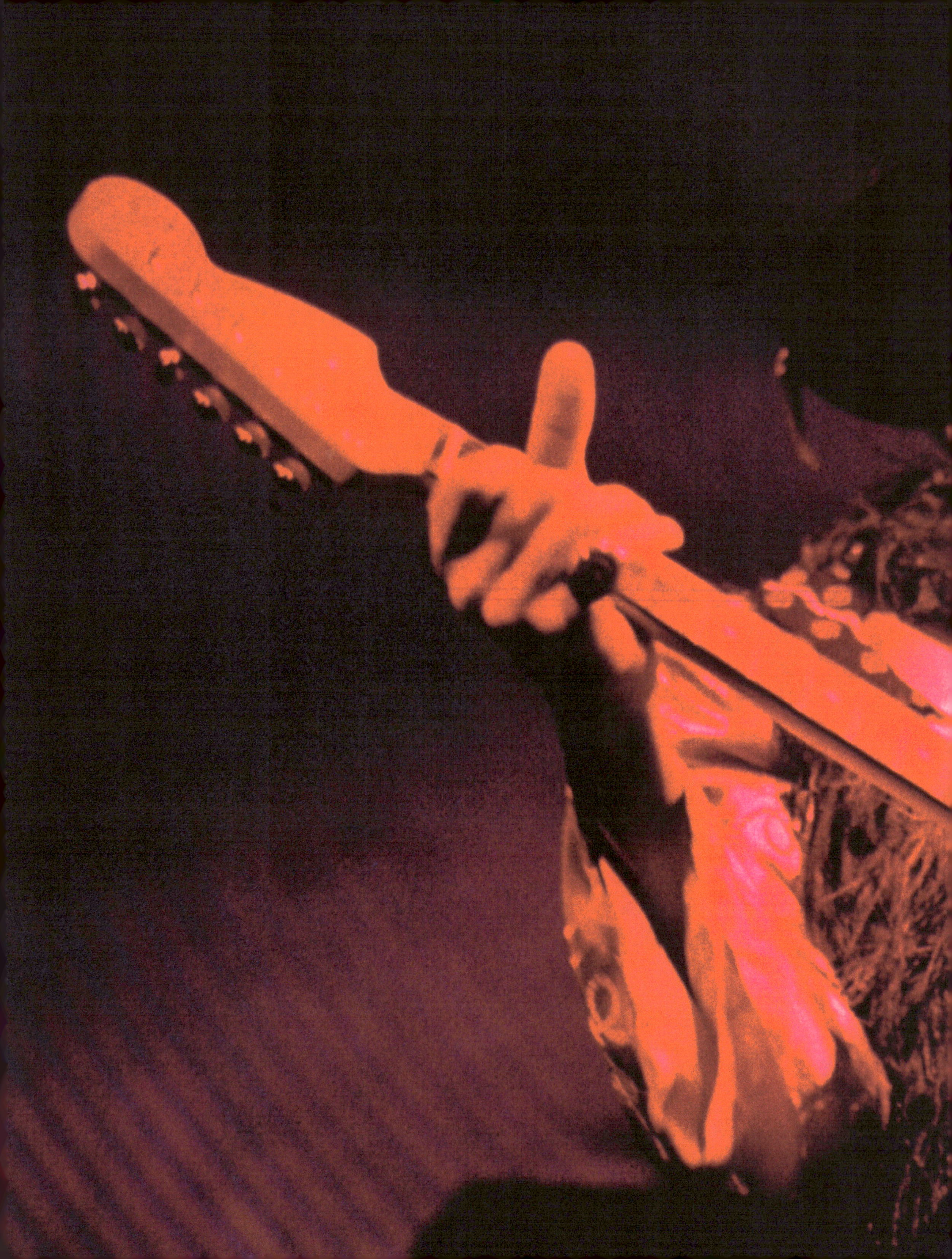

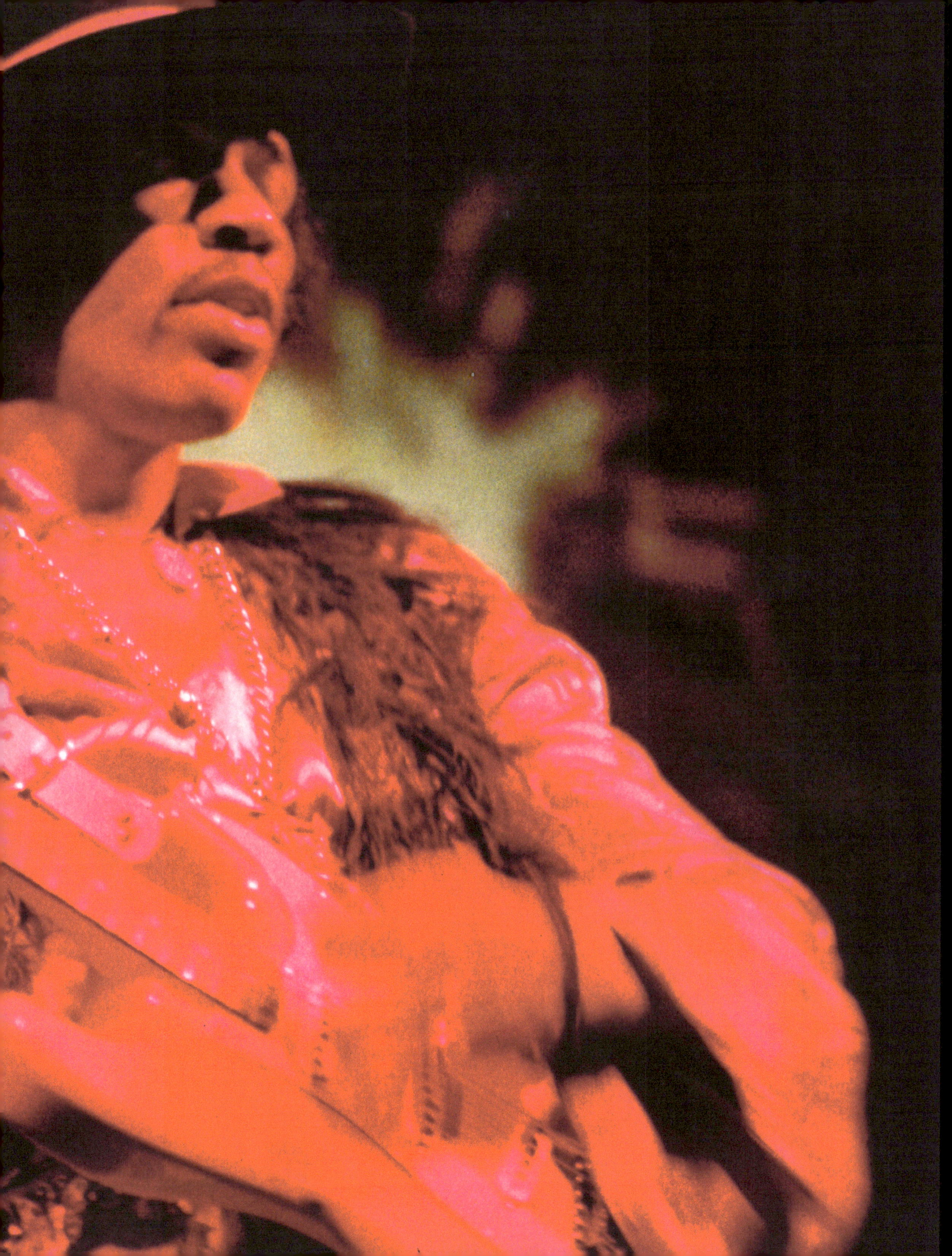

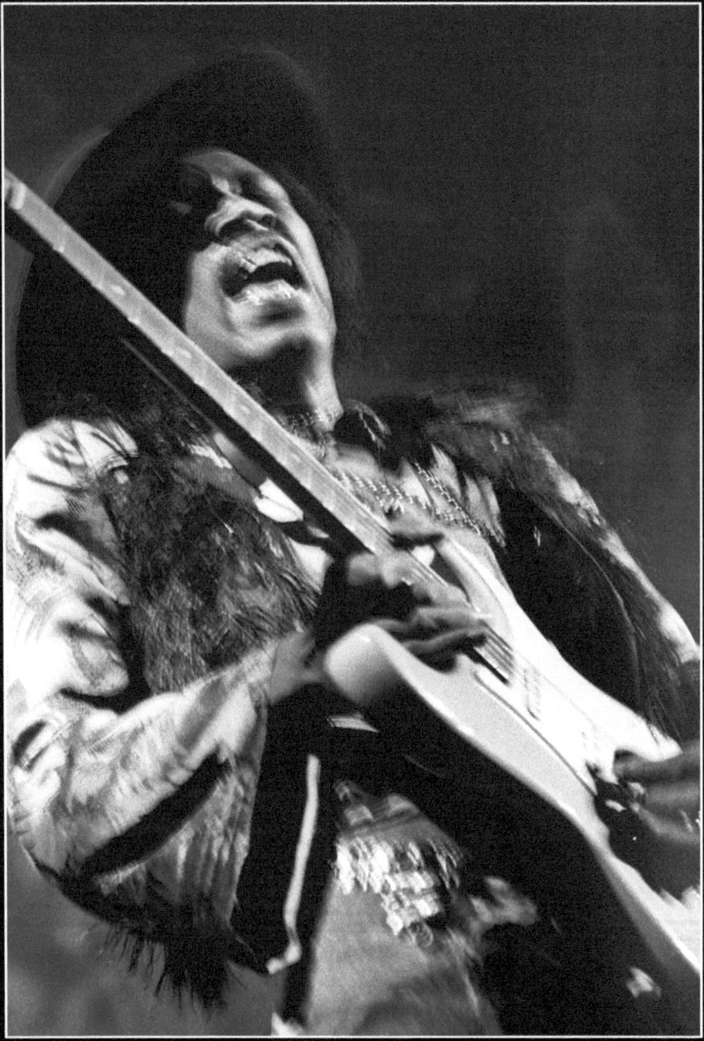

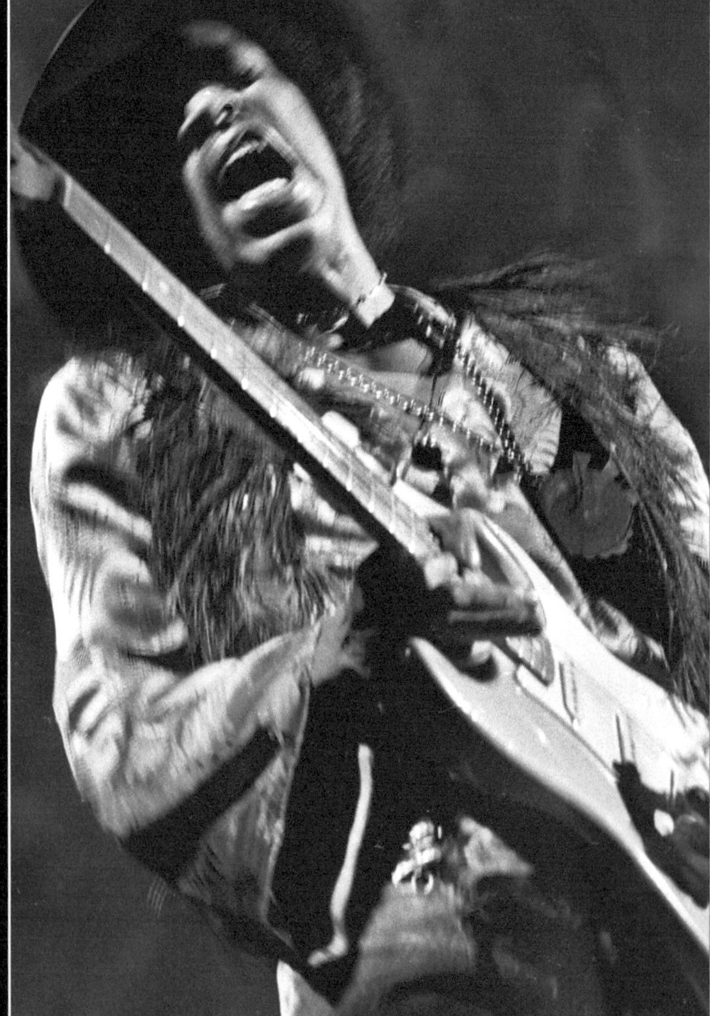

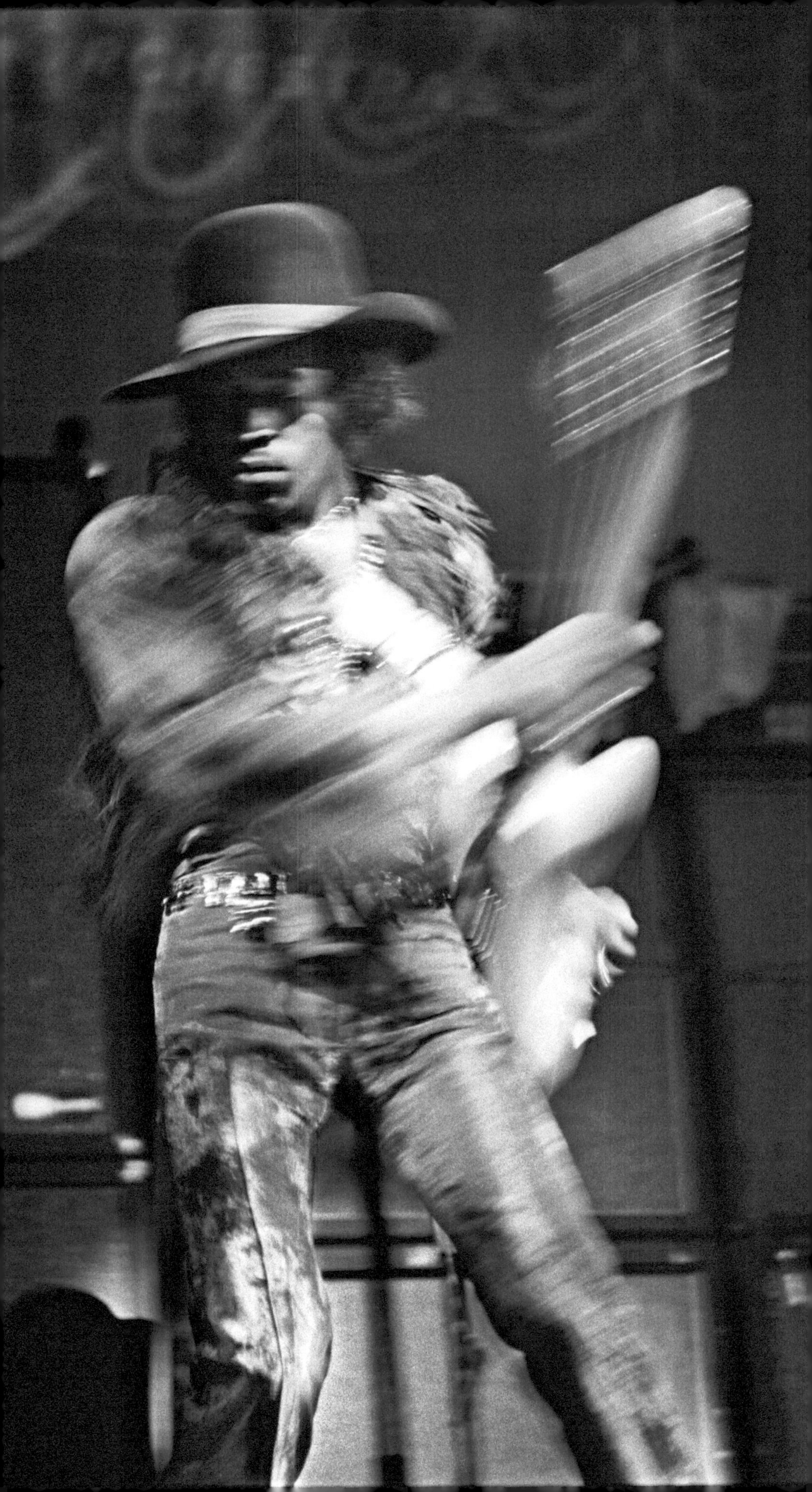

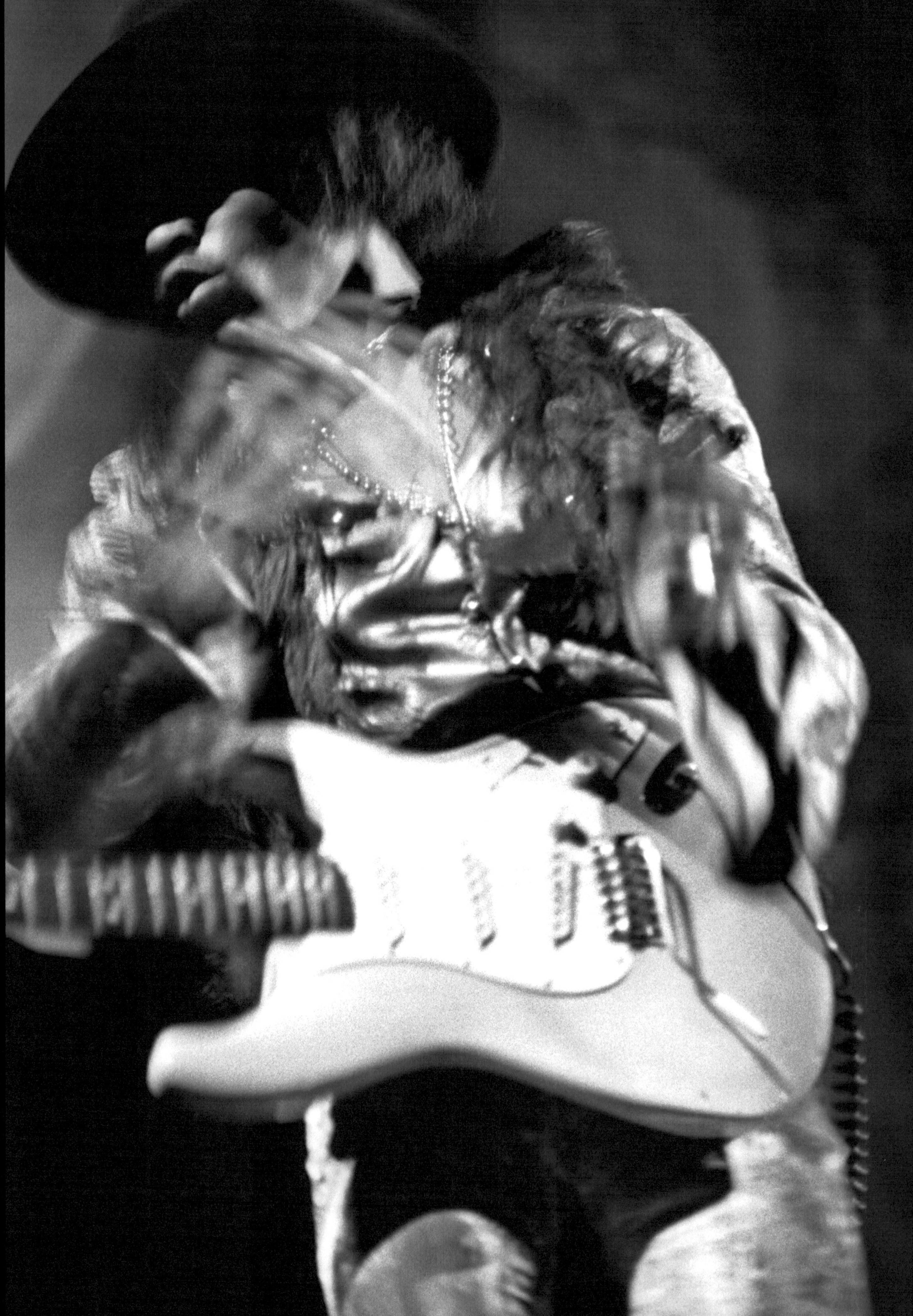

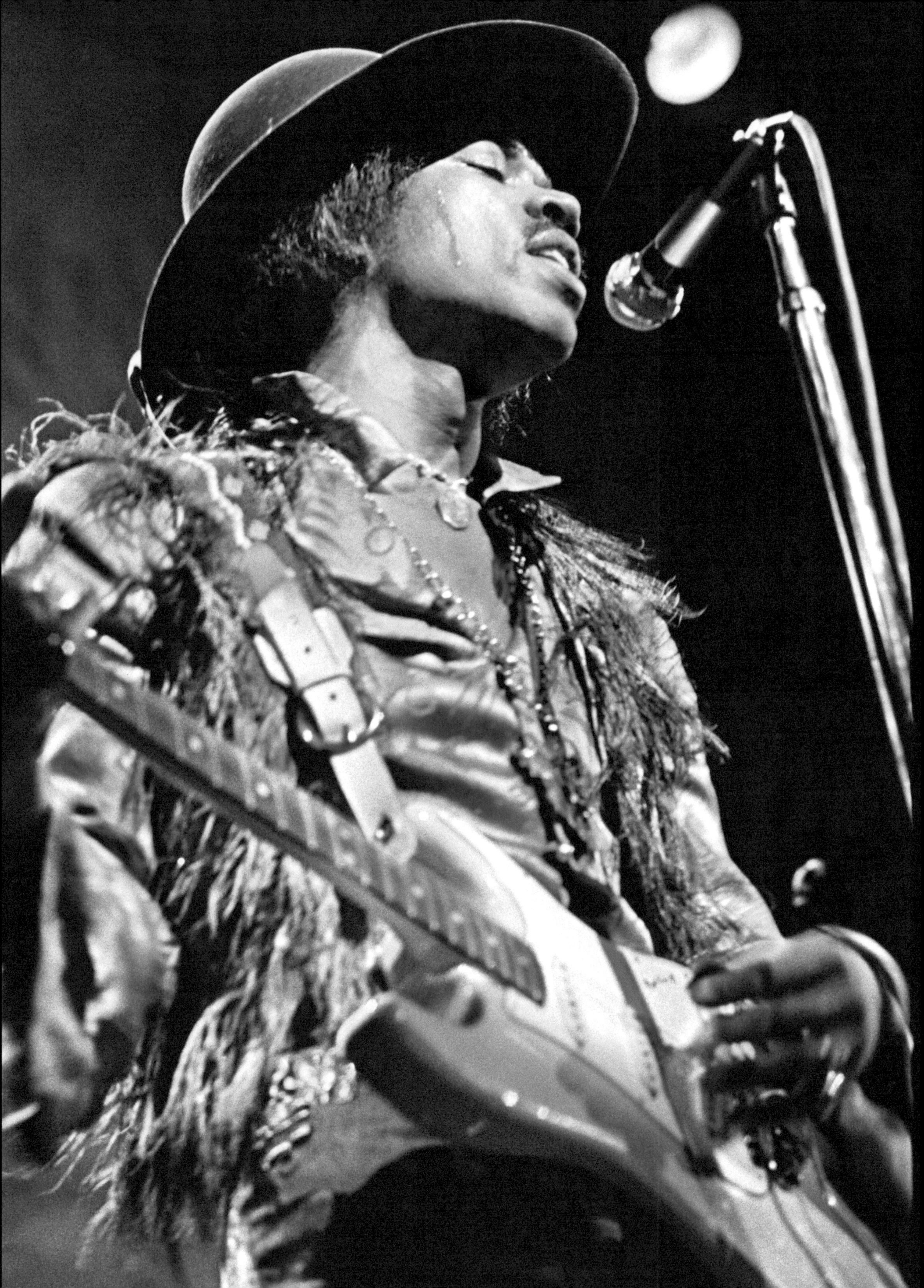

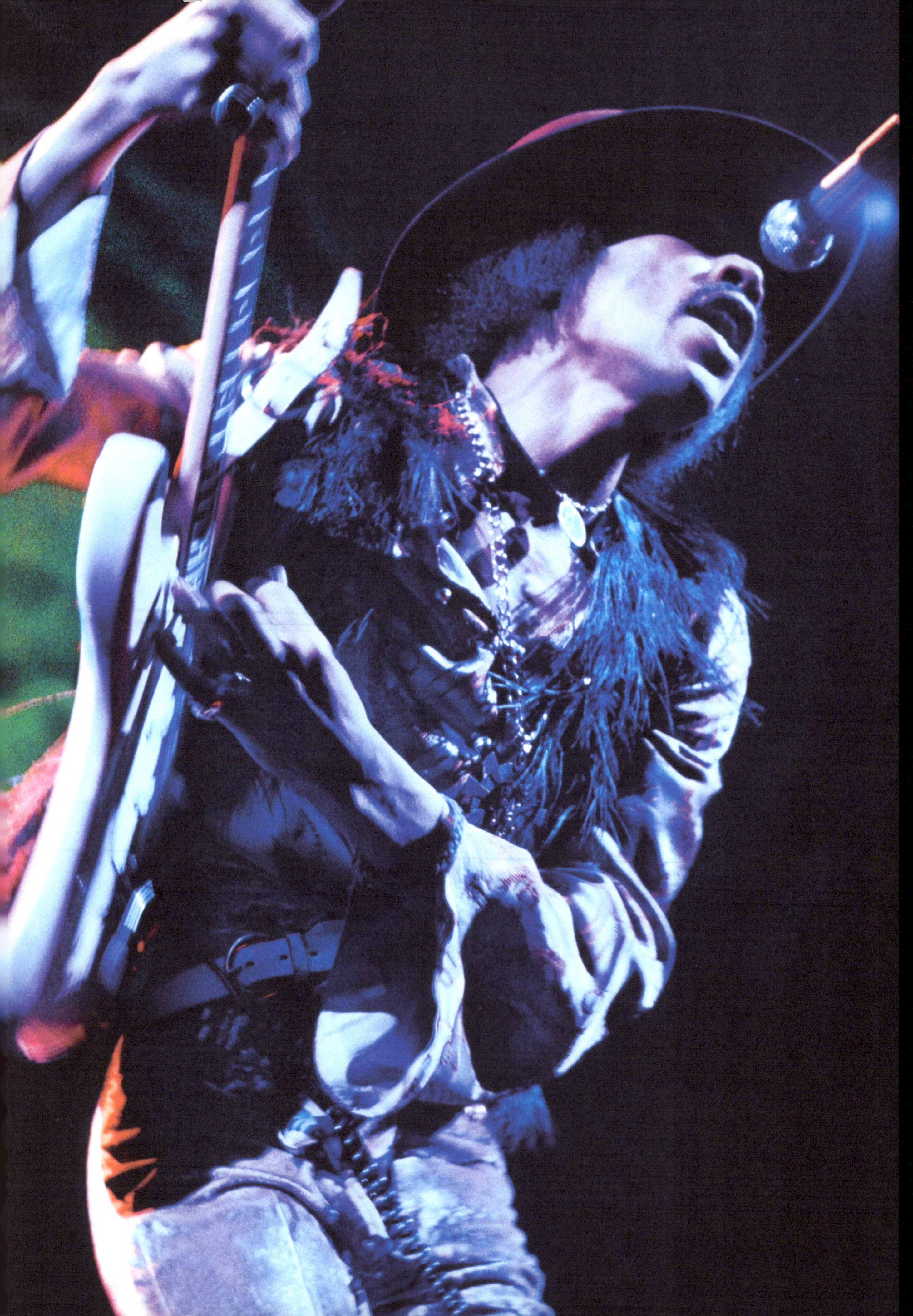

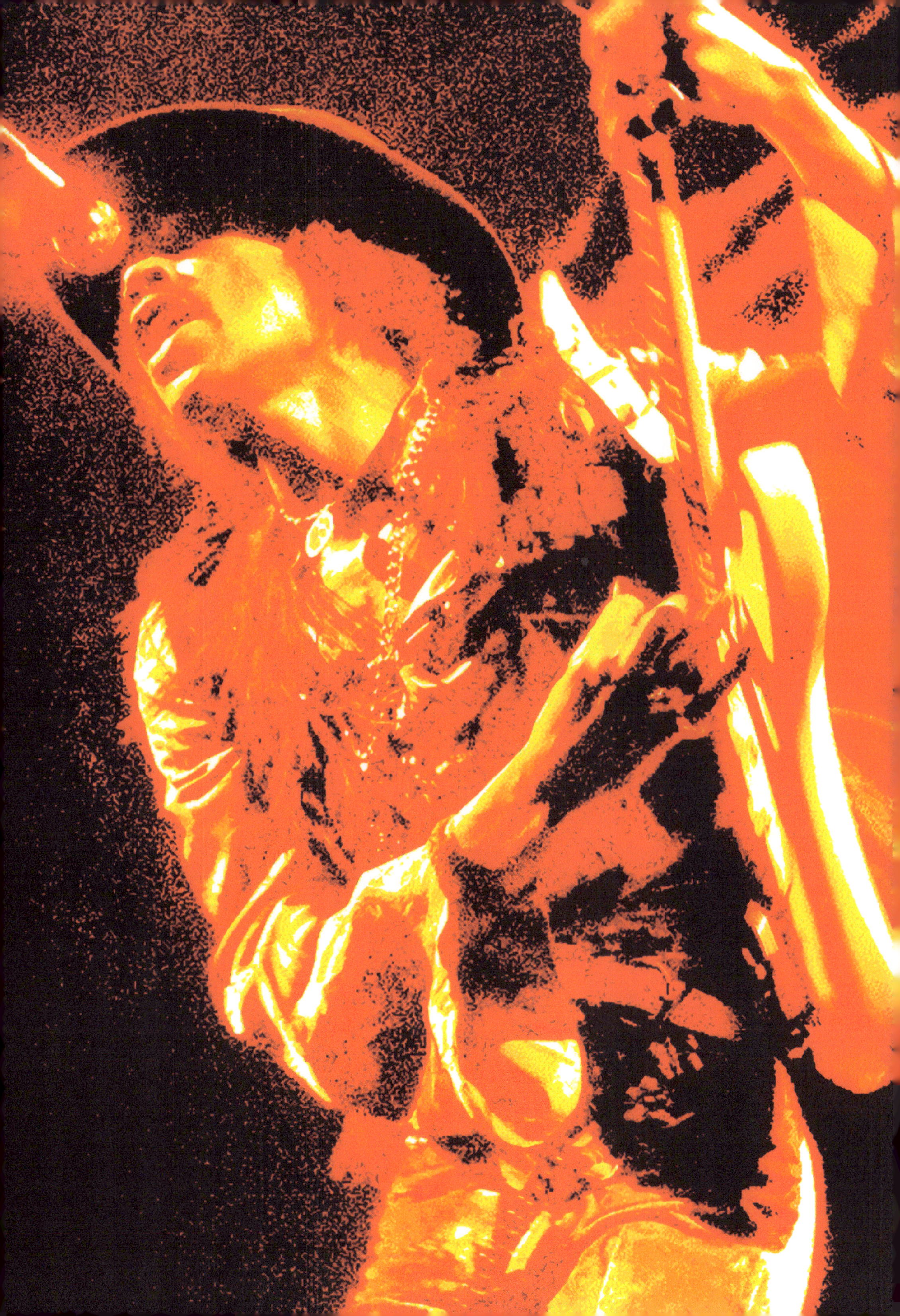

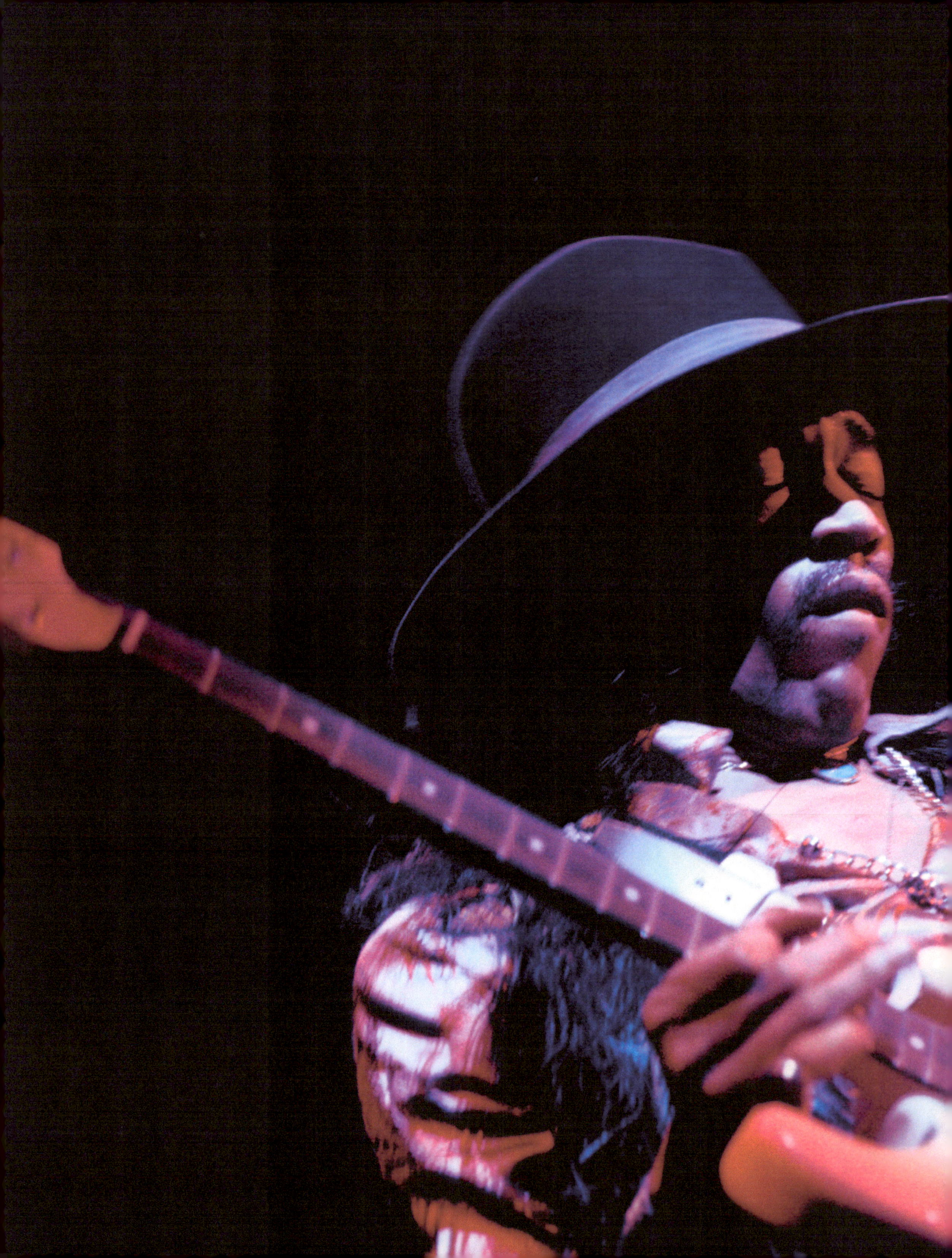

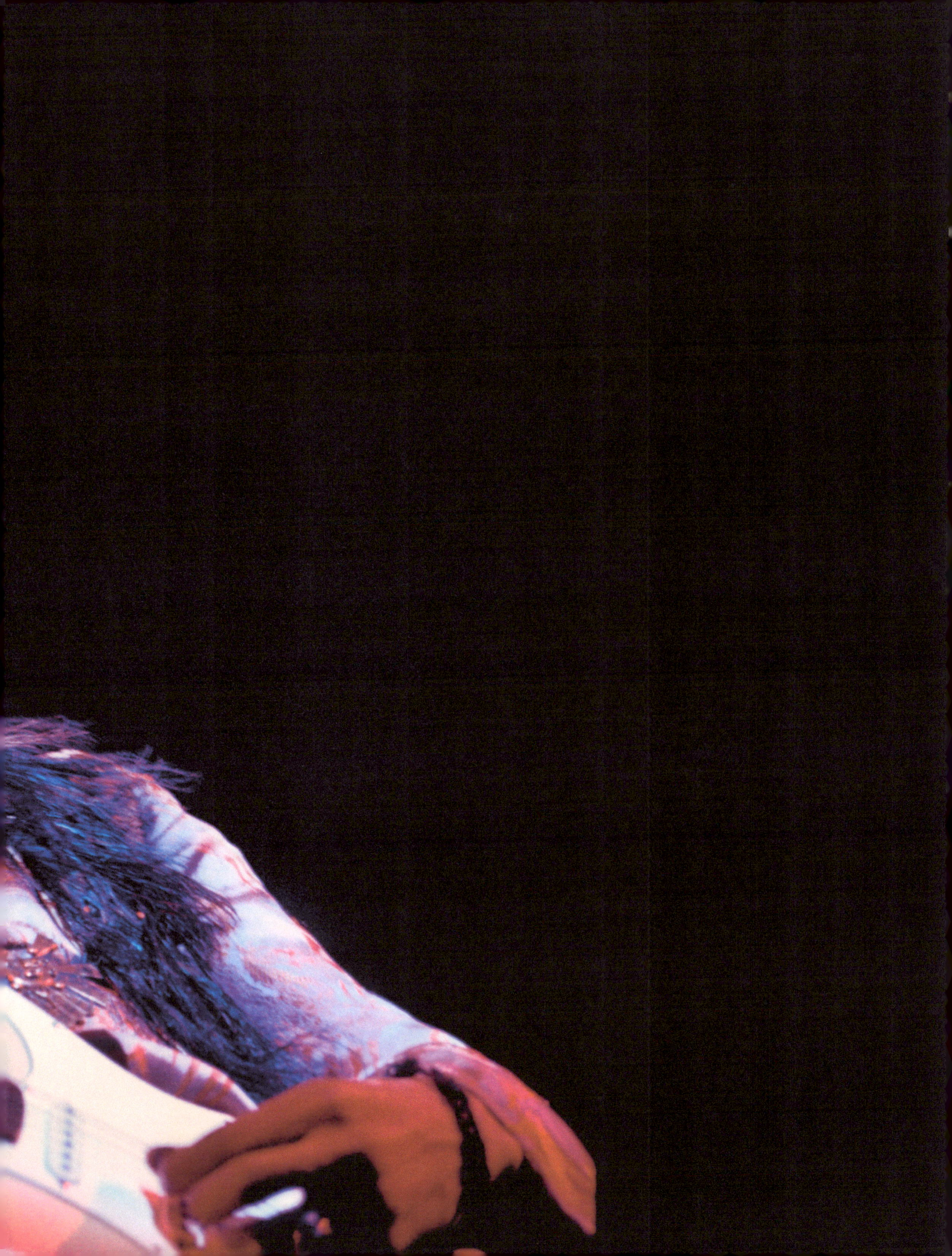

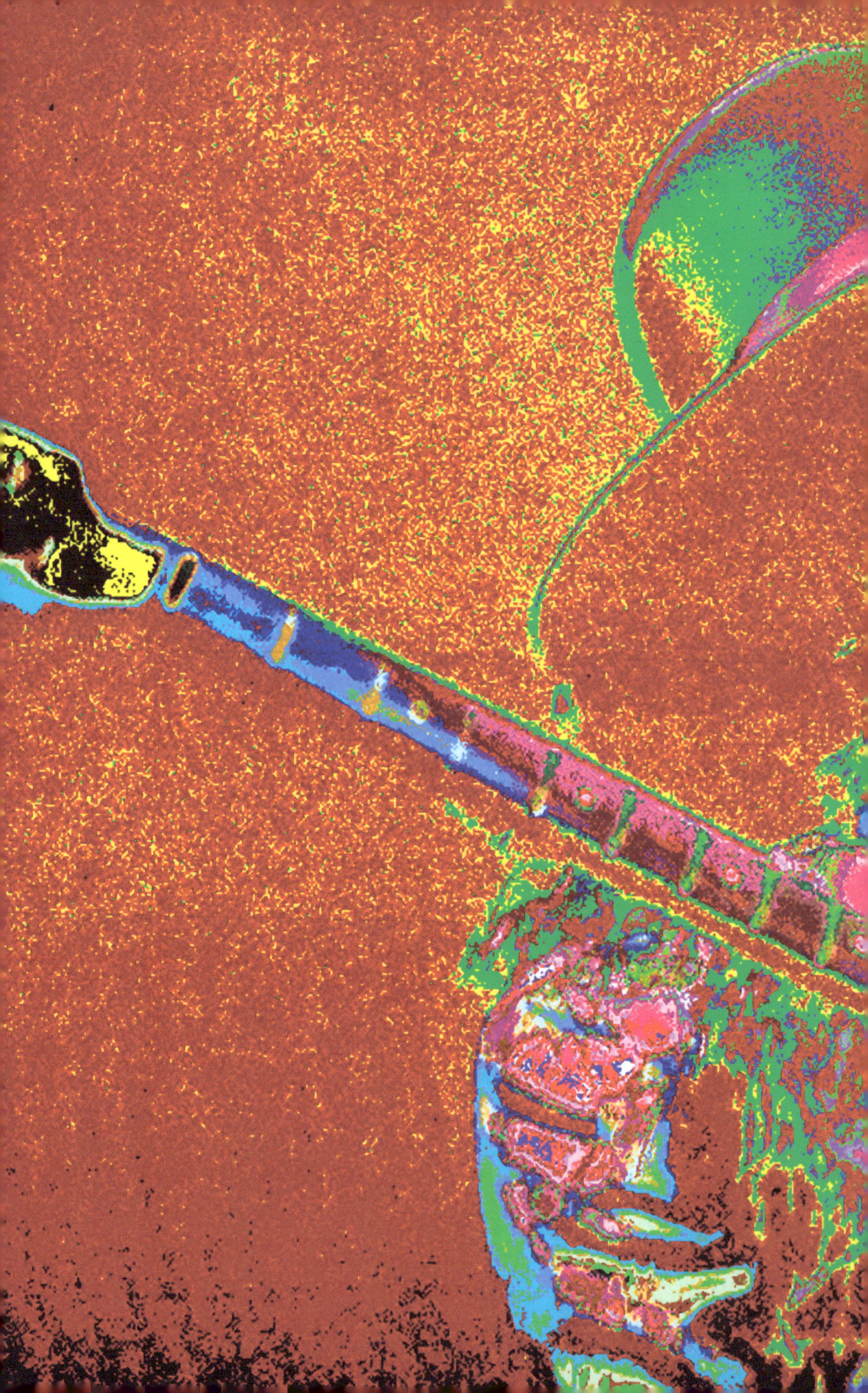

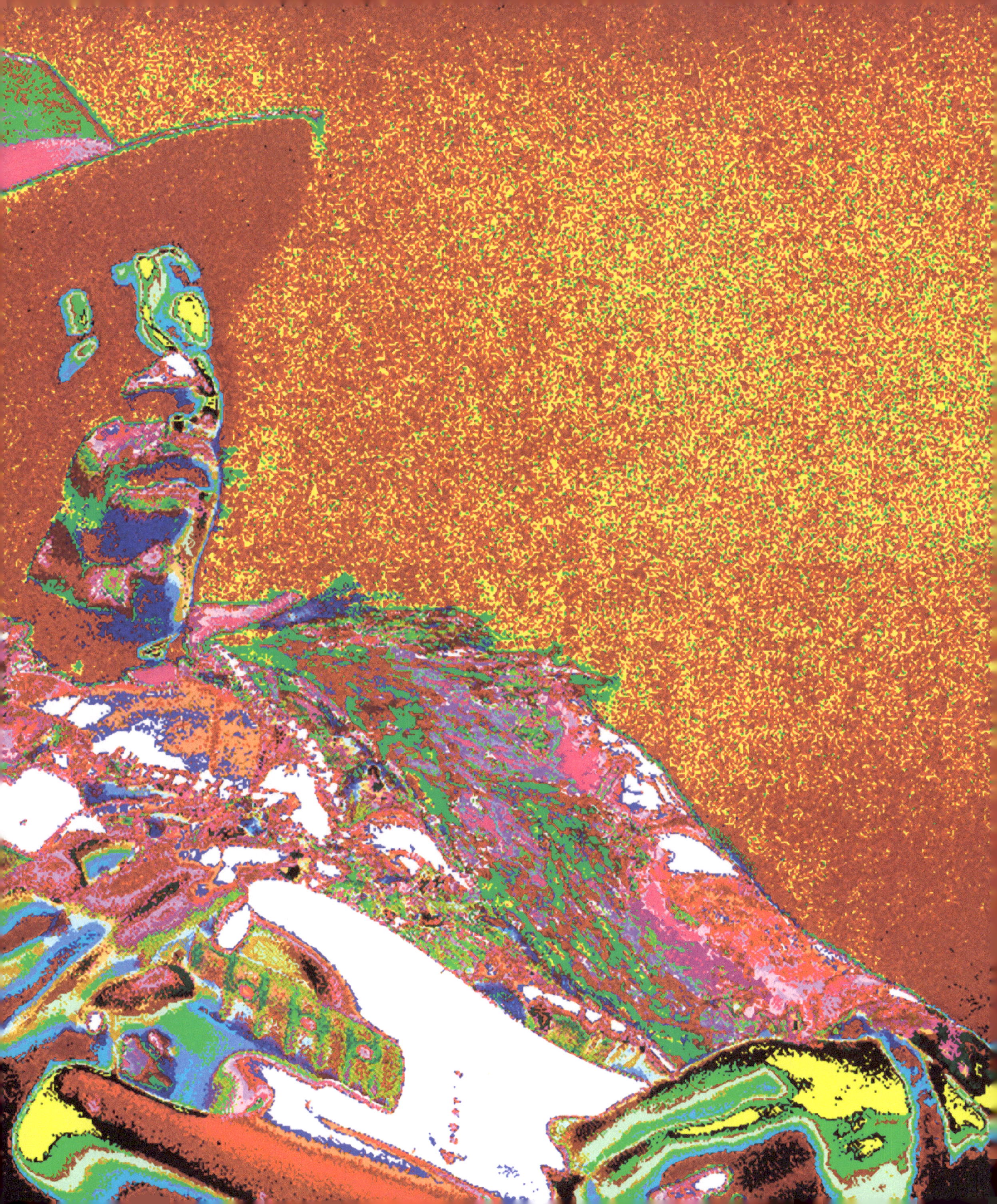

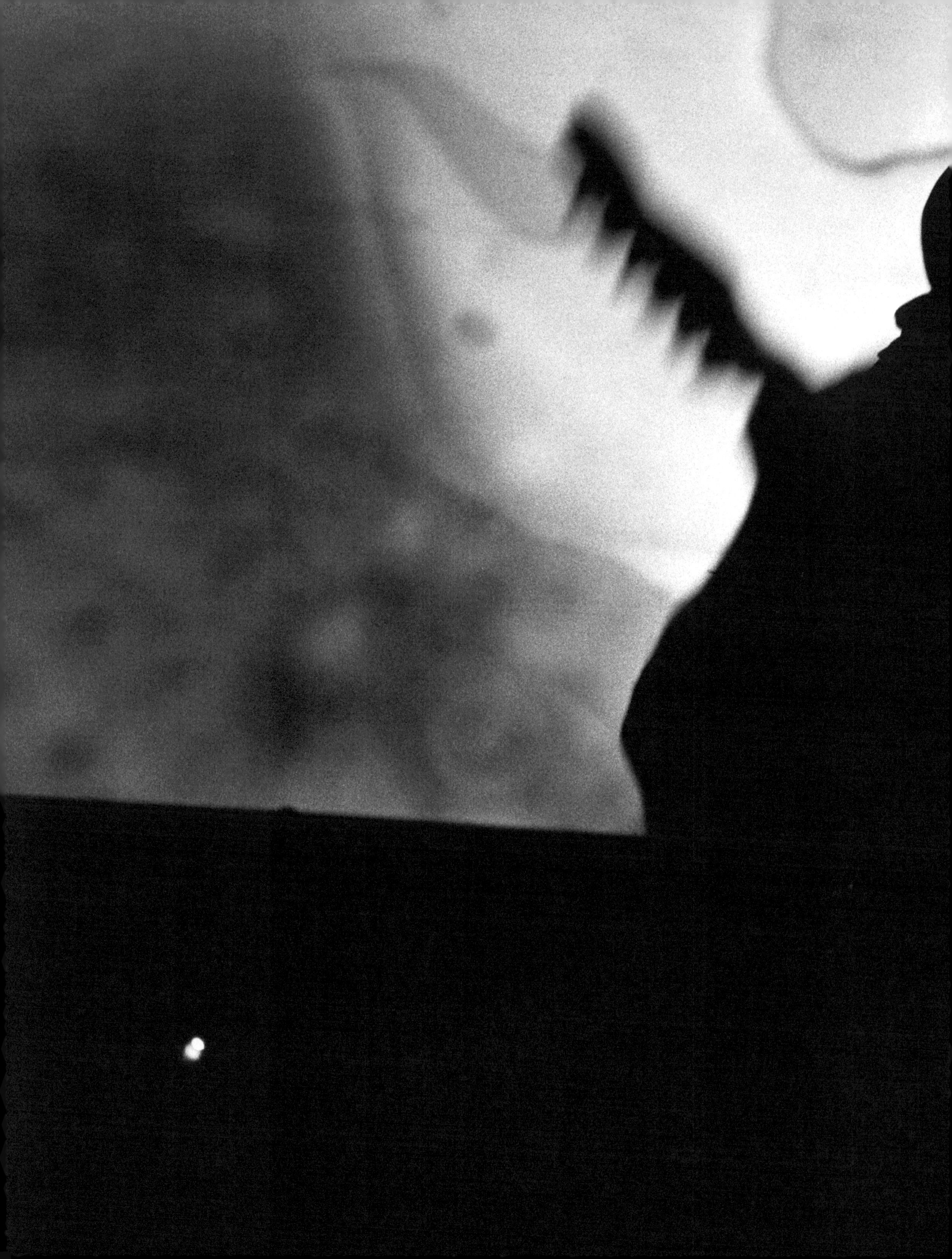

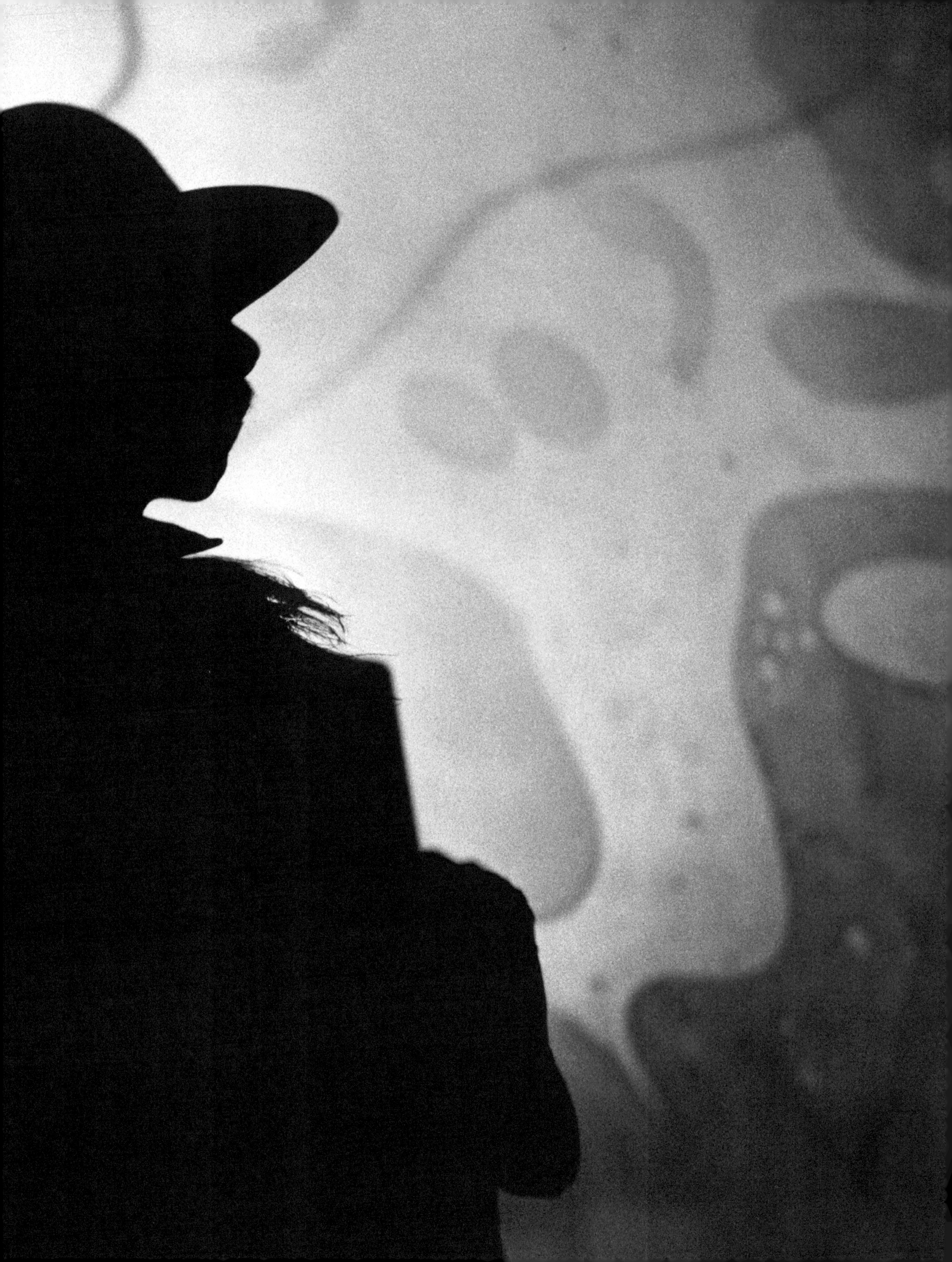

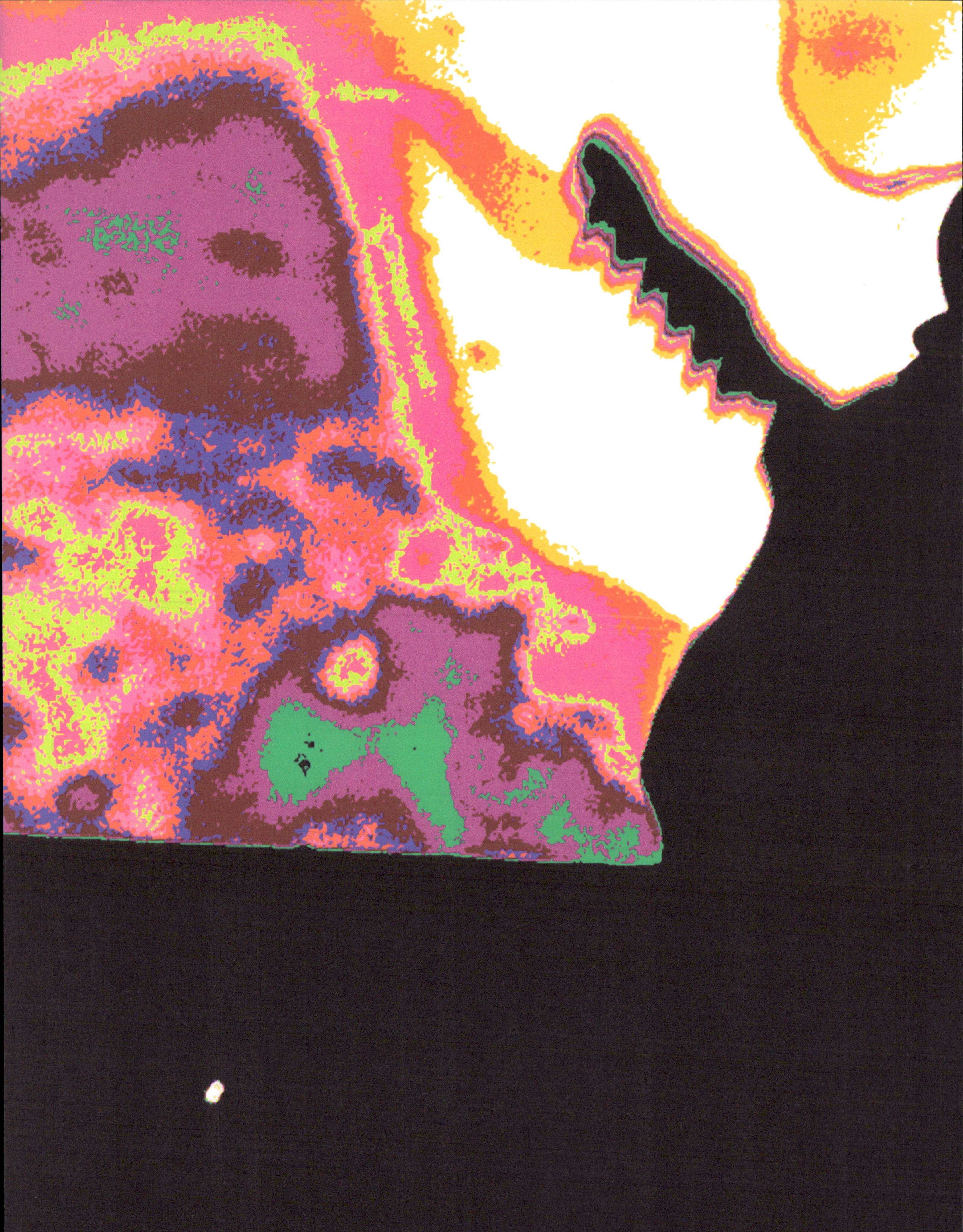

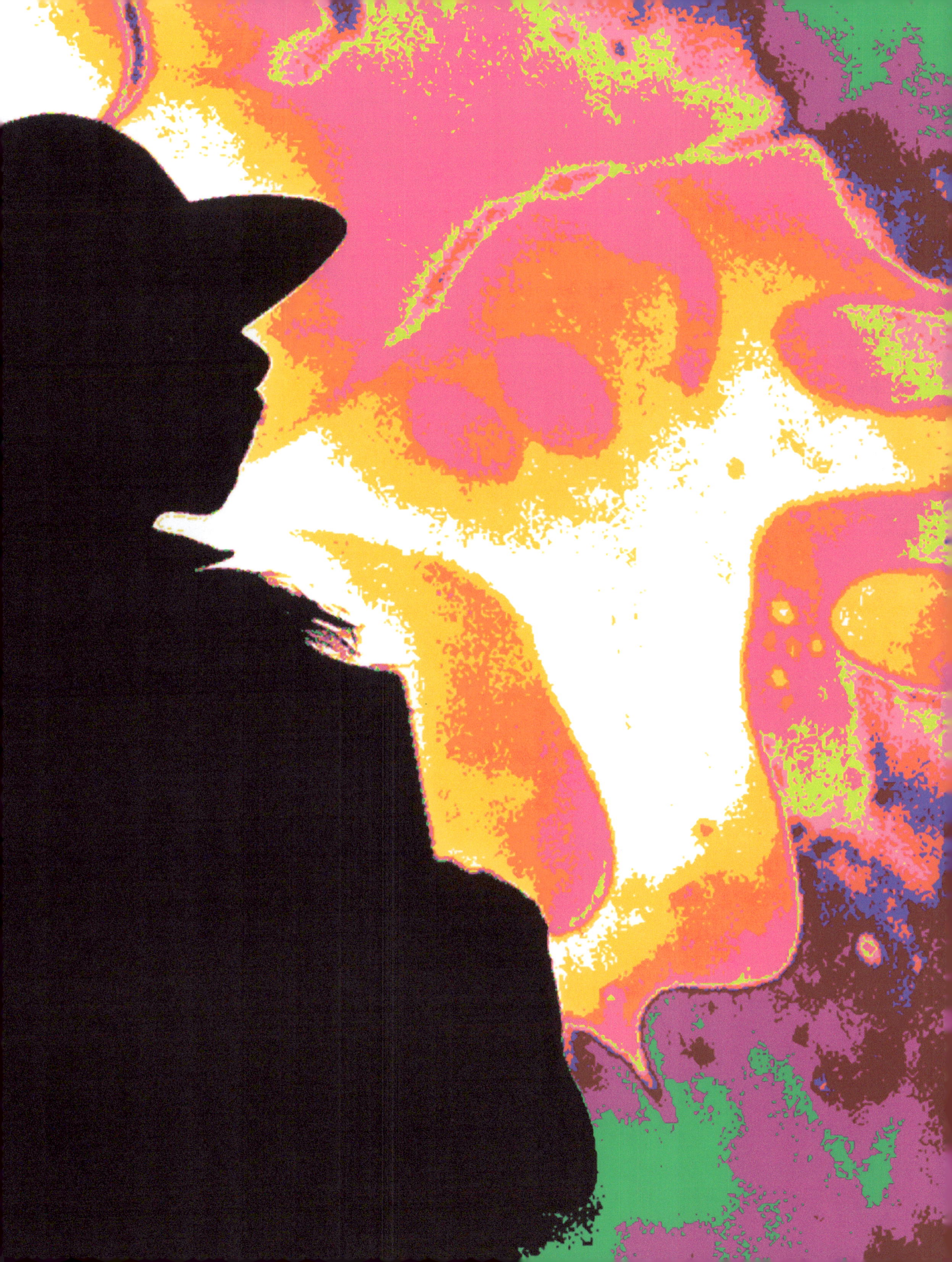

Faded Flowers
Al Aronowitz
www.blacklistedjournalist.com

I had to talk Miles into going to Jimi's funeral with me. What the hell, I told him, it was only a few days before he had to be out on the Coast anyway and besides, the exposure would be good for him. There'd be a lot of press there. "I don't like funerals," he rasped. "I didn't even go to my mother's funeral." In the end he made the plane, Miles, with his hairdresser, Vinnie, and Jacki, a girl he had picked up out of the crowd at LaGuardia Airport one day. "She had just come off a plane getting into the city," he explained, introducing her, "and I was catching a plane to fly out on a gig. I saw her on the other side of the lobby and I called her over and told her to get on the plane with me, and she did."

. . . They buried Jimi Hendrix in the bright afternoon in a hilltop cemetery amid the sobs of people who hadn't really known him for years. It was a cloudless day. Several hundred kids watched from behind ropes. Seattle had never understood Jimi, and now it had to open its earth for him . . .

Miles and Jimi hadn't known each other too long, but in the shot time they did they had gotten pretty tight. Jimi was one of those kids who had grown up worshipping Miles as Miles kept getting younger. For as long as Jimi could remember, Miles had been a legend to him, and it was only when he felt secure enough as a legend himself that he came to sit at Miles' feet and ask Miles to record an album with him. Miles said shit, he'd be happy to do the album but he wanted $50,000 for it. For that much of his soul, he wanted that much money. Like when Sidney Poitier tried to hype Miles into doing the sound track for some movie, he told Miles not to worry about the money because the movie would make Miles famous. "Man," Miles answered, "I'm already famous!'" Miles was a big influence on Jimi. Miles is a teacher. But Miles learned something from Jimi, too, learned something about rhythms and something about phrasing and something about the rock and roll lifestyle. It was Jimi who became the final inspiration to move Miles to renounce the classical forms of jazz, many of them created by himself, and to start playing the rock halls. Miles knew how to stay as young as any kid. What he wanted to find out was how come a kid like Jimi could make fifty thousand dollars in one night when Miles still couldn't make ten.

. . . It had been nine years since Jimi left the vast green valleys that had sent him off in search of a home he could not find and now his flesh was back amid the airplane factories, the strip mine quarries, the salmon canneries, the steel mills and the breweries that had tried to trap him. . .

Steve Paul was on the plane. Steve, the underground entrepreneur who had used to run the Scene at 46th Street and Eighth Avenue, New York's most outrageous cellar rock club. Steve, host to the stars, had become a friend and confidant of Jimi's through the long, hangout nights at the club, where Jimi used to go to get so drunk and drugged he couldn't stand up any more, and still he'd get onstage and jam till dawn. Steve was on the plane with guitar star Johnny Winter, the Albino Whisper, a tender, quiet, bashful sweetheart until he starts picking those Texas roadhouse blues. Steve and Johnny were married, in the music business sense. Steve was Johnny's manager, guiding him to the big time, Mr. Yokel and Mr. Brash. And then there was John Hammond Jr., who had hired Jimi to play in his band in the Village way back when. It was while Jimi was playing with Johnny Hammond in the Cafe au Go Go, that Chas Chandler and Michael Jeffrey first laid eyes on the spectacle of Jimi wasting a guitar. Chas was a big star then, one of the Animals. Mike was the Animals' manager. It was from Johnny Hammond's band that they lured Jimi away to England to become the World's Next Superact.

. . . Jimi had become one of the greatest stars ever to make music, one of the sweetest poets ever to make the language dance. But back in Seattle all they could bury was the memory of a little black kid who used to play on his father's two-stringed ukulele.

On the plane it was like a party. It was a party. We were all Jimi's invited guests, flying First Class according to his wishes as expressed by Mike Jeffery, Jimi's manager, in collaboration with Mike Goldstein, Jimi's press agent. We seat-hopped all the way to Seattle, with the two Johnnies getting off on getting to know about each other and me tap dancing between Steve and Miles, who was holding court at the table past the airliner's galley, the Black Prince. I guess the real reason I talked Miles into coming was for his company. When we got to Seattle, Steve, the two Johnnies and I went to the Hilton Inn at the airport, a motel, where Jimi was paying for our rooms. Miles grabbed a limo to the Washington Plaza, the brand new glass, steel and granite showpiece in the center of town, where he checked Vinnie, Jacki and himself into a luxury suite. He said he'd pay for his own rooms.

. . . At the Dunlap Baptist Church on broad Rainier Avenue in south Seattle, Mrs. Freddie Mae Gautier, a woman Jimi knew well enough to call Mom, presided at the services and read from Jimi's liner notes on the Buddy Miles album, "Expressway to Your Skull": "The express had made the bend, he is coming on down the tracks, shaking steady, shaking funk, shaking feeling, shaking life. . . the conductor says as they climb aboard, small we are going to the electric church, the express took them away and they lived and heard happily and funkily ever after and---uh---excuse me but I think I hear my train coming.". . .

At the motel, our party from the New York plane was amalgamated into a bigger party. There had been other planes from L.A. and London' and even Barry Fay, Jimi's promoter in Denver, had jetted in for, the mourning. All of Jimi's sidemen were there, all the roadies and managers who had ridden his express, all the little people along the way, like myself, who had given Jimi whatever breaks they could, the flagmen of his career. Even Nancy, Mike Jeffery's ex old lady, who loved to draw. Jimi hadn't passed her by either. In the end, he wrote her letters. His first album after he died had her drawing of him on the cover.

In the pews were rock stars Johnny Winter, John Hammond Jr. and Mitch Mitchell and Noel Redding, both of whom had played with Jimi in the Jimi Hendrix Experience. Drummer Buddy Miles, who also had played with Jimi, collapsed at the coffin when it was opened for the invited guests to pay their last respects. Inside the coffin, Jimi looked waxen and unreal. . .

Jimi wouldn't have loved the Party so much as the idea of it, hosting a bacchanal on his own grave. I mean there was plenty of feasting, drinking, smoking, rapping, snorting and picking, with most of the musicians sitting in with the local rock group in the night club downstairs. But none of the girls took off any clothes in public and even the craziest of the English contingent kept their manners-zipped up. Steve Paul and I had a good time day-dreaming about Miles and Johnny Winter touring together. Otherwise, we were less than the pirates we would have been if Jimi was there. Jimi, the eternal swashbuckling buccaneer, with his plumed hats and ferocious presence, and I sometimes could even imagine a sword hanging from his wide leather belt. Not that the party

was lame; but what was missing was Jimi. The biggest excitement came out of a rumor spread by Press Agent Goldstein to the effect that Paul McCartney was going to show up, due in any second. The rumor turned out to be so effectively planted that the next day one of the wire services reporters sent a story out to the world saying that Beatle Paul did indeed attend the funeral.

...Outside the church there was a crowd of 200 including reporters, photographers, and TV crews. A half dozen police cars were parked across the street. A dozen police motorcycles were waiting around the corner. Twenty-four limousines lined the curb. . .

In Jimi's absence, Mike Jeffery played host. For Mike, this consisted mainly of sitting in a booth in the coffee shop so people who recognized his power could come over and pay their respects. Of course, aside from his power there was very little to recognize in Mike. I mean he certainly didn't stand out in a crowd, and, unless he was trying to hustle you, you'd have trouble detecting any personal dynamism from his direction. People who talk about him say geniality did not come easy to Mike except for profit. Me, I found Mike easy. His problem was that he suffered from an occupational hazard among music business managers known as eclipse. When you're managing a star, the bigger he grows, the bigger the shadow he casts over you.

The Mike I knew constantly seemed surprised by his success, except in the safety of his own small circle of hand-picked friends. Mike learned early that when you're a star, nothing you say is wrong. Mike, on the other hand, would rather say nothing than say something wrong. If this made him a cold fish, it also made him a better shark. Being invisible helped Mike become a hit manager. But what he wanted most was to be recognized. At the Hilton coffee shop, everybody took a turn coming over to his booth. The party was for Jimi but it was Mike's party. Still suffering from eclipse, he presided over the festivities without ever getting in the way of them. Even beaming, he dimmed his light with the cloak he was most comfortable in: anonymity. To turn Jimi's funeral into a circus was to Mike's advantage because he had a legend to maintain for profit. Jimi still had an album or two in the can and maybe a movie. Jimi was dead but he was still product. I never doubted Mike knew what he was doing. For him the party at the Hilton may have been his finest moment. A year or so later he went down in an airliner that fell into the sea off the coast of Spain.

. . . Alongside the coffin were a dozen floral sprays, including one six-foot white and lavender guitar made up with velvet strings. The family had chosen Dunlap Baptist Church because Jimi's nine-year old stepsister, Janie, was a parishioner there. Janie, in fact, was the only member of Jimi's family who went to church. . .

In the morning I took a cab into the center of the city to meet Miles in his suite at the Washington Plaza. Miles always travels First Class. He had sent Vinnie on ahead to the Hendrix house in south Seattle to fix up the family's hair-dos for the funeral. Miles will give you his last buck, too, if he cares for you. We sat and had breakfast and then Miles dawdled as he dressed. He was almost ready by time the chauffeur got back from taking Vinnie to the Hendrix house. On the ride there, we talked about how Seattle runs at a pace 20 years behind New York; it felt like we were back in the '50s, maybe even the '40s. It was a comfortable town, but you could see where it could get boring. At Jimi's father's house, a small, gray, one-family home in a mixed residential district, I couldn't keep track of all the members of the family I was introduced to. Jimi's father looked just like Jimi. And Devon was there, dressed in black with a black veil over her face. "Are you playing the merry widow already?" Miles asked her.

. . . James Marshall Hendrix was born in Seattle on November 27, 1942, to James Allen and Lucille Jetter Hendrix. Mrs. Gautier read from the church podium: "His mother preceded him in death. . . Jimi, as he later became known to all his fans, felt that his hometown did not afford him the outlet to express himself with his musical ability. . ."

Devon was the closest thing Jimi had to an old lady. He left her a widow's pension in his will. She was one of the most beautiful and sensuous of the groupies and one of the most successful, too. I first met her in the '60s, I forget with whom, but whenever a rock star came to New York, the chances were you'd find Devon in his hotel room. They used to recommend her to one another. Her sex was overwhelming. Somebody once told me she was a teacher and I used to wonder of what. In all the times Devon and I talked to each other, we really never got to know what we were all about. We would just gossip. It got to be amazing how her relationship with Jimi survived. She could never totally belong to anybody, just as Jimi couldn't, but somehow they came to depend on each other. I saw her a few times after Jimi died. She was hard not to love. I was writing a column for the New York Post in those days and she kept asking me, "When are you going to write a column about me?" And I kept saying to her, "When are you going to do something?" I think it was in March of 1972 that she took an OD and died.

On the podium Mrs. Gautier read from a poem sent anonymously by a student at Garfield High School, where Jimi had been kicked out for sassing a teacher who had become annoyed because he was holding hands with a white girl. "So long, our Jimi," Mrs. Gautier recited. "You answered the questions we never dared to ask, painted them in colorful circles and threw them at the world. . . they never touched the ground but soared up to the clouds. . .

After Jimi's funeral, I went to Monterey for the pop festival and then spent some time with Miles in San Francisco, where he was working a club.

I was backstage at Winterland with the Grateful Dead and the Jefferson Airplane when word came that Janis had been discovered dead in her motel room in L.A. I didn't know what it all meant then and I still don't know, but even as I write this there's a moth beating itself to death on the electric bulb of my lamp. And in a little plastic cup on my desk near my typewriter there are two dried out flowers, faded blue, from Jimi Hendrix's graveside.

Are You OK?
by Tommy Fuller

After Jimi's closing set at Woodstock, I was heading out... cold and damp, wrapped in a blanket and really suffering from sleep depravation. I saw a group of people getting into a black Chevy Bel Air four door. I recognized Billy Cox, the bass player for Jimi Hendrix. Two women with him were getting into the backseat. One looked like Jimmy's girlfriend.

I stood there watching them and then Jimi approached the car. He looked over at me and asked, "Are you okay?" It took me a little while to answer, "yes" so Jimi, obviously concerned, asked me again, "Are you sure?" I answered "yes" again. He smiled, gave me the peace sign, then got in the car and drove off. I still remember Jimi's face as he said that to me. I couldn't believe that Jimi Hendrix took the time to make sure I was OK. It still amazes me to this day.

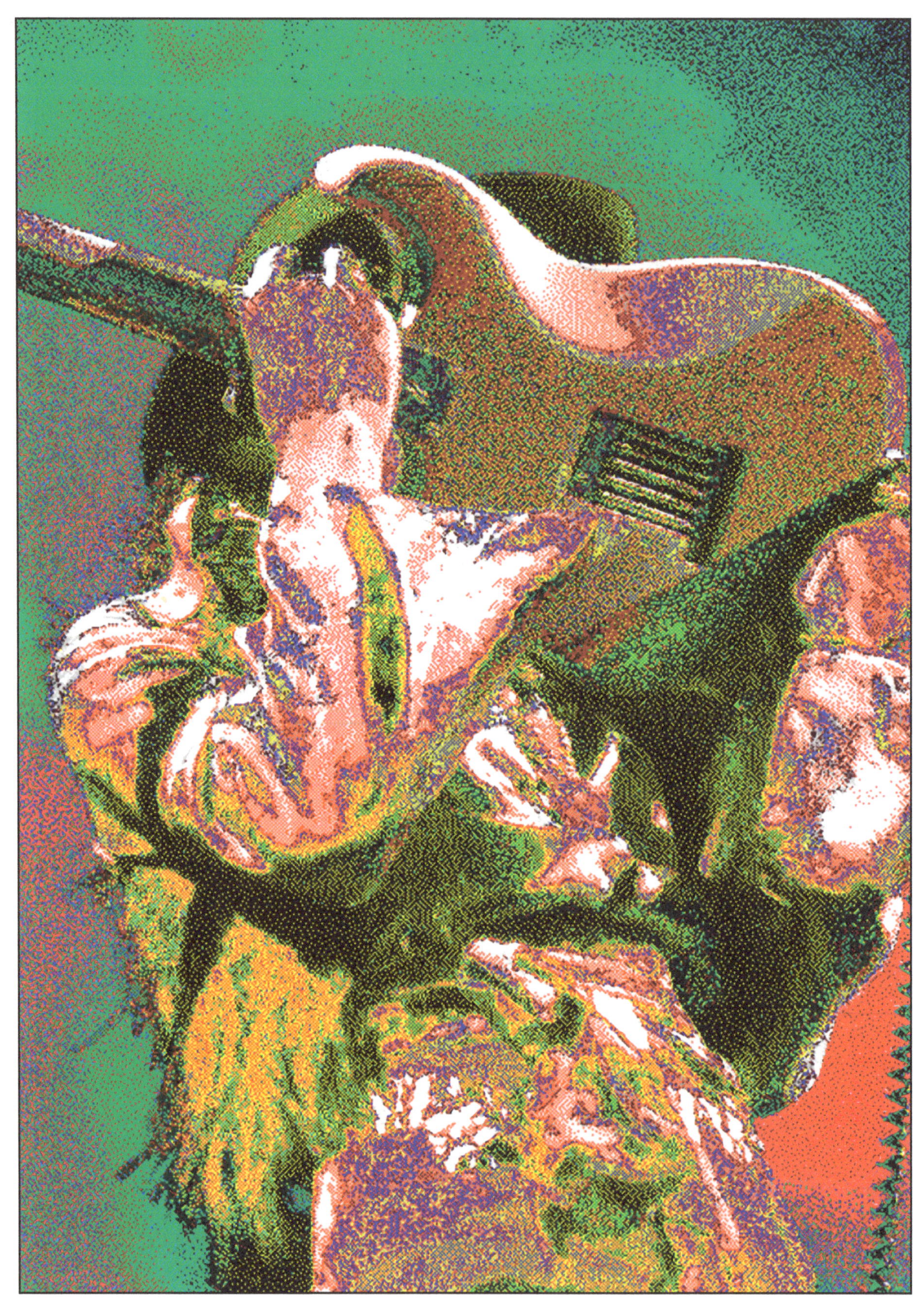

TEXT ON COLORIZATION
v7a